MW00479002

Praise for

Star Guide
to
Weddings

"Marriages have horoscopes too! Each has its own personality, purpose, and needs. Whether you're planning the perfect wedding or hoping to nourish the marriage you already have, this little book is an indispensable guide. Decades of experience with weddings and brides make April the premier astrologer to consult before and after the 'I do's.' April's writing is fun, her stories engaging, and best of all, her insights and advice are right on."

—Dana Gerhardt, *The Mountain Astrologer*

"April's elegant book is the kind of astrological gem I most treasure. Without pretense or wordiness, she distills a tremendous amount of wisdom and helpfulness down into simple images and guidelines. And after a quarter century of marriage myself, I can promise you that everything she says about the Capricorn relationship is spot-on! I suspect couples married under the other eleven signs will agree."

Star Guide
to
Weddings

About the Author

April Elliott Kent has studied astrology for over thirty years and has practiced professionally since 1990. She has contributed to *The Mountain Astrologer, Wholistic Astrologer, Llewellyn's Moon Sign Book,* and *MoonCircles,* an online magazine. Her work has also appeared on Beliefnet.com and AOL Horoscopes. She is a member of the International Society for Astrological Research, the National Council for Geocosmic Research, and the San Diego Astrological Society.

Star Guide

to

Weddings

YOUR HOROSCOPE
FOR LIVING
HAPPILY EVER AFTER

APRIL ELLIOTT KENT

Llewellyn Publications
Woodbury, Minnesota

First Edition
First Printing, 2008

Book design by Joanna Willis
Cover design by Lisa Novak
Cover illustration © Tammy Shane/Langley Creative
Interior illustrations © Pepper Tharp

Portions of this work have been adapted from the article "Summer Wedding Astrology" by April Elliott Kent, previously published by Tarot.com. Used with permission.

Llewellyn is a registered trademark of Llewellyn Worldwide, Ltd.

Library of Congress Cataloging-in-Publication Data
Kent, April Elliott, 1961–
  Star guide to weddings : your horoscope for living happily ever after / April Elliott Kent.—1st ed.
    p. cm.
  ISBN 978-0-7387-1169-0
  1. Astrology and marriage. I. Title.
  BF1729.L6K46 2008
  133.5'864678—dc22
                          2007038502

Llewellyn Publications
A Division of Llewellyn Worldwide, Ltd.
2143 Wooddale Drive, Dept. 978-0-7387-1169-0
Woodbury, MN 55125-2989, U.S.A.
www.llewellyn.com

Printed in the United States of America

Contents

Acknowledgments

The process of creating a book is like marriage: it's a collaboration that makes us better than we could hope to become on our own. Thanks to Sharon Leah, who introduced me to Llewellyn; Lisa Finander and Stephanie Clement, who persuaded me to write this book; eagle-eyed editor Karl Anderson, a charming gentleman who didn't let me get away with *anything*; Michelle Krueger; Courtney Kish; Bill Krause; and the brilliant artists who designed such charming clothes for my baby: Joanna Willis, Lisa Novak, Tammy Shane, and Pepper Tharp.

Personal thanks to my colleagues Dana Gerhardt, Steven Forrest, Diane Ronngren, Philip Brown, Jeffrey Kishner, and Natori Moore for indispensable advice; Tim Tormey and Claudia Fernety for cheering me on; and Drew, Mari, Kathy, and Chuck, for honing my wit. Thanks most of all to Jonny, who taught me everything I know about marriage—with love, patience, and a twinkle in his eye.

Welcome to the Book

*I*f you're like most modern-day humans, you know a little bit about astrology. At the very least, you probably know your Sun sign and a few of its alleged characteristics. Probably you know a little something about your spouse's Sun sign too, and maybe even how well your two signs supposedly get along. But did you know that your marriage also has a Sun sign—based on the day you were married?

And why not? After all, every marriage has a personality all its own, with quirks, charms, and a distinctive style of operating. As certainly as the personality of a friend or loved one intrigues, inspires, and occasionally exasperates you, so does the personality of your marriage.

A Marriage Is More Than the Sum of Its Parts

I'm sure you've known a friend whose personality changed radically from the moment the wedding ring slid into place—the shy bookworm who began hosting lavish dinner parties, the couch potato who took up hang-gliding, the fashion plate who gave up acrylic nails because her husband doesn't like them.

A partner exercises enormous influence over the way you see and behave in the world. A partnership with someone who validates and supports you can draw out reserves of strength and confidence you didn't know you possessed. But a relationship with someone who uses his influence or insight negatively can undermine these same reserves, crushing your spirit under the weight of derision or indifference.

The same is true of marriage. Put a lively, fiery Leo and a chatty, sociable Gemini into a pragmatic, ambitious Capricorn marriage and watch the sober, serious cloak of that sign cast its influence over these two vivacious individuals. They may draw maturity and support from Capricorn's stern influence, but it's also likely that they will find the cast of their Capricorn union a bit stifling, even depressing, from time to time.

Astrology doesn't cause this kind of interaction between two people—it simply describes it. The compatibility between two people remains a mysterious thing, a wild synthesis of chemistry and Freudian psychology, physiology and spirit. A skilled astrologer who specializes in relationship astrology can certainly guide you through the labyrinth of possibilities, even do a fair job of identifying the sore spots, strengths, and weaknesses in your marriage.

But astrology is an imperfect art, whether it's used to understand individuals or the marriages they build together. The intangible force that eludes astrological analysis—and is perhaps a more reliable indicator of relationship than anything else—is the determination by both people in the marriage to make the relationship work. Surely it's that kind of determination that led you to pick up this book in the first place!

What This Book Reveals about Your Marriage

- *What is your purpose for being together?* Is yours a Capricorn marriage like the one between George H. W. and Barbara Bush, destined to perpetuate a dynasty? Or perhaps a Leo union like the one between passionate artists Frida Kahlo and Diego Rivera, a fiery, tempestuous romance that inspired some of Kahlo's most famous work?

    Every marriage has potential strengths—the ability to go with the flow, perhaps, or to come up with innovative solutions to tough problems, or stay fixed to a specific purpose. There is something that your marriage, at its best, **wants to become**— its potential best self, emphasizing all its strengths and few of its flaws. Often, family and friends grasp this potential "best self" even before it's evident to the two of you!

- *What does your marriage need? What keeps you together?* Money, children, conversation, sexual attraction, spiritual convictions, business, romantic love—all are potential motivations for two people to build a life together. What's yours? What are the main qualities that sustain your marriage and feed your intimacy with one another? Understanding your marriage sign is a key to understanding this potential.

- *What is your marriage style?* Some signs are stubborn and inflexible; others have a hard time staying on topic. Some dwell in the world of intuition and emotions, others are pragmatic and stoically resigned to life in the here and now. Understanding the style of your marriage sign can help you resolve differences and capitalize on what your marriage *is* rather than worrying about what it *isn't*.

- *What does your marriage want to help you become?* Marriage, as people with a gift for positive spin like to say, is a wonderful opportunity for personal growth. Living day to day with an intimate partner will test and stretch your own limitations and boundaries—and some days, you'll feel testy indeed.

Even the happiest of marriages has a shadow side, a mischievous trickster who sits on your shoulder and whispers in your ear nasty, poisonous things about your partner. There almost inevitably comes a moment when you look at the person you married, the person you have pledged to cherish above all others, and just feel … irritated. Must your beloved be so stubborn, so willful, so wishy-washy, so selfish, so clingy? The wiser question, and one astrology is uniquely well-suited to answering, is something like this: what is it in you that needs to change in order to better understand and love your partner—and continue to grow into a better and wiser version of yourself?

Finding Your Marriage Sign

This book is designed with all levels of astrological knowledge in mind, ranging from basic to advanced. Each chapter is devoted to one of the twelve signs of the zodiac. Each describes what a marriage "born" under that sign might be like, including that marriage sign's approach to money, to children, to sex, to career success. To find your marriage sign, simply locate your wedding date in the list below. Note: If you were married on a day when the Sun is changing signs, consult an astrologer to calculate the position of the Sun at the time of your wedding.

Aries	March 21–April 20
Taurus	April 21–May 21
Gemini	May 22–June 21
Cancer	June 22–July 23

Leo	July 24–August 23
Virgo	August 24–September 23
Libra	September 24–October 23
Scorpio	October 24–November 22
Sagittarius	November 23–December 21
Capricorn	December 22–January 20
Aquarius	January 21–February 18
Pisces	February 19–March 20

BUT WHAT IS A "SIGN"?

Although we know that the Earth revolves around the Sun, it looks from our perspective as though the Sun is moving across the sky throughout the year against the backdrop of the zodiac. Picture a sort of cosmic wallpaper speckled with stars, the kind that, when you were a kid, would have kept you busy for hours when you were home sick in bed, looking for pictures of animals and heroic figures in its patterns.

These groups of fixed stars, the constellations, came to be associated with figures from legend and myth. As the Sun appeared to move through each of these constellations at the rate of about one per month, certain things were happening on Earth. For instance, when the Sun moved through Aries, the spring planting was underway, animals began to mate, and life force was generally in full and riotous bloom. And so we think of the Aries season of the year a time of new beginnings, sexual energy, and general liveliness.

WHY THE SUN?

The Sun is the central figure in our solar system, so vital to our lives that, like oxygen, we give it little thought. Our seasons, our days, and the clock itself take their meaning from our movement around the Sun. In astrological symbolism, the Sun represents the core of a thing, the point in a psyche or a society or a marriage around which everything else revolves. So the Sun's sign on the day you were married gives vital information about your purpose for being together. Have you come together to create a family (Cancer), explore new worlds (Sagittarius), or provide a secure foundation for others (Taurus)?

Each sign of the zodiac has acquired a rich patina of folklore, evolved over centuries of observation and tradition, including descriptions of a sign's "style." Each sign is associated with qualities of leadership, tenacity, or flexibility; of passion, sensitivity, practicality, or analytical ability. If the Sun's sign at the time of your marriage has a very different style than the Sun's sign at your birth, you will have some adjustments to make. Either the marriage will have to adapt to make room for your individual mode of expression, or you will have to compromise your needs with those of the marriage. Most likely, it will be some combination of the two.

MARRYING UNDER THE "WRONG" SIGN

There really is no "wrong" sign under which to marry. Some signs, such as Libra or Taurus, really are very compatible with society's concept of marriage as a stable union of equals who form a relationship for reasons of both practicality and affection. Others, such as Scorpio or Aries, may challenge society's ideas about matrimony—but that doesn't make them bad marriage signs. Each sign takes a different approach to marriage, and each has something unique to teach us about forming an intimate partnership with another person.

In the last chapter of this book you will find guidelines for choosing your most compatible marriage signs, based on your own Sun sign. But please, take those recommendations in the spirit intended—as a general guideline. Astrology, and people, are more complicated than Sun sign symbols alone would suggest. Whether or not a sign appears on some list, there may be all kinds of reasons that marrying during a particular season is absolutely right for you.

You have chosen to wed . . . and in an age when half of all marriages end in divorce, that is an act of tremendous optimism and faith. My hope is that this little book may in some way help you better understand the character of the union you are creating … a living, breathing entity that defies the best efforts of anyone to pigeonhole or stereotype it.

Any marriage can work, if both people want it badly enough. That is the simple truth. Nothing in this book should be interpreted as an indictment of any marriage that is undertaken in consciousness and faith, with the warmest of intentions and the determination to succeed in the difficult task of loving each other for a lifetime. For the marriage you are creating together every day, you have my deepest respect, and my warmest wishes for consciousness, strength, and great happiness.

The Aries Marriage

(MARCH 21–APRIL 20)

Famous Sun-in-Aries Marriages

Mary Pickford and Douglas Fairbanks (March 28)
F. Scott and Zelda Fitzgerald (April 3)
Christopher and Dana Reeve (April 11)
Grace Kelly and Prince Rainier (April 19)

❧✦❧

Are you a fan of bodice-ripping romance novels, in which noble lords resembling Fabio charge around on white horses rescuing demure but lusty maidens?

Have I got a marriage for you!

Romantic and dashing, impulsive and inspiring, the Aries marriage has a certain reckless glamour. You appear to be madly in love with one another, even (or especially) when you're arguing about something—which is often! The course of true love doesn't necessarily run smooth when it leads one into an Aries marriage—but it sure as hell is exciting. There is the rescue motif, just for a start: it's hard not to fall for someone who shows up to untie you from the railroad tracks just before the oncoming freight train can flatten you.

But quite beyond the knight-on-a-white-horse, damsel-in-distress romanticism, the Aries marriage brings out the superhero in both of you. Regardless of your individual natures and talents, when you enter into an Aries marriage you become leaders, pioneers, and survivors. Whether you lead a nation like Grace Kelly and Prince Rainier, start up an influential corporation like Mary Pickford and Douglas Fairbanks (who, along with Aries Charlie Chaplin, founded United Artists studios), or transform personal tragedy into social activism like Christopher and Dana Reeve, others come to admire you. You aren't the sort of couple to sit around and meekly hope for life to give you permission to do what you want to do. Together, you inspire one another to create your own opportunities and to set out bravely into the wild unknown.

The Aries Season

The Sun enters the sign of Aries at the vernal equinox and marks the official beginning of spring, a season associated with birth and new beginnings. During this season, Christians celebrate Christ's resurrection at Easter, while Jews celebrate Passover, marking the exodus from Egypt and their symbolic birth as a people. Even the weather is lively in spring. Cold and warm air circulate and collide, resulting in the most severe weather events of any season, with flooding, tornadoes, and thunderstorms common. And let's face it: a soundtrack that features thunder, lightning, and wind doesn't exactly spell "smooth sailing" so much as "batten down the hatches, and full speed ahead!"

In Greek mythology, Aries (the Romans identified him as Mars) was the son of Zeus, the king of the gods, and was the god associated with savage war. Though Aries' half-sister Athena was also worshipped as a war deity, her approach to warfare emphasized strategy, while Aries favored violence and brute force. Some cynics might observe that a god of war is an appropriate ruler for marriage; these are people who joke about "the war between the sexes," and whose humor masks a certain grim conviction that men and women just can't get along.

But the astrological Aries is just as likely to emphasize the courage, leadership, and determination of the mythical god as its angry, violent face. Individuals born with the Sun in Aries tend to march to the beat of their own drum, take chances where others hesitate, and excel in leadership positions.

Likewise, a marriage that begins during the Aries season tends to produce a couple who are viewed as pioneers among their families and friends—the first to try anything that's new, scary, or unconventional, and in particular those things that accepted wisdom holds cannot be done. Certainly no one suspected Prince Rainier of Monaco would take a Hollywood actress for his Princess, nor that Grace Kelly, an Oscar-winning actress, would relinquish her career in show business to reign over a tiny country far from her native land.

How It Begins: The Aries Wedding

Even though Aries' symbolism springs from a fairly bloodthirsty mythic legacy, Aries in fact has an extremely courtly, idealistic, swooningly romantic side in the mold of Lancelot and Guinevere, Helen and Paris. (Although perhaps it's not so weird when you consider that both these great, courtly romances ended with a great deal of bloodshed and heartbreak!)

The brash, impatient energy of Mars/Aries demands acknowledgement from those who marry during his season, and in fact there may be an expediency in your decision to marry now—perhaps for tax or insurance reasons, or even because there is a child on the way (the stereotypical and, for Aries, appropriately named "shotgun" wedding). Yes, Aries will find his voice one way or another, so if there is a way you can honor the nobler aspects of the warrior god—his courage, valor, and dashing spirit—within the context of your wedding day, it's smart to do so. The alternative, such as temper tantrums at the reception, are so much less appealing.

For couples currently serving in the armed forces, a wedding with military honors (dress uniforms, raised swords) is an ideal invocation of Aries' warrior spirit. A Catholic couple may choose to honor a warrior saint, such as St. Joan of Arc, in their ceremony. One couple I know who married in early April "got hitched" at a wedding chapel with a Wild West theme (six guns optional, presumably)! Another option for pioneering Aries wedding couples is simply to hold your ceremony in a place that is not a traditional wedding venue. Be the first to marry on the rooftop of the restaurant where you had your first date!

Aries likes fire too, so if the weather is still a bit crisp you can honor the Aries/Mars energy by exchanging vows in front of a roaring fire. Candlelight is a reasonable substitute, but you'll need lots of candles— preferably red, the color sacred to Aries—to do justice to the passionate nature of this sign.

As in traditional Chinese wedding ceremonies, all shades of red are considered good luck for the Aries wedding couple, as well as white. You might even consider wearing a red silk bridal gown, or a more traditional white gown but with bright red shoes and flowers. Bridesmaids will look lovely in red dresses or ivory with a sprigged pattern in red, and groomsmen with red boutonnieres.

Red and white blooms, including some with bold scents, are an excellent choice for bouquets, boutonnieres, altars, and centerpieces. Carnations, poppies, tulips, geraniums, honeysuckle, and hollyhocks are all associated with Aries and are mostly available in shades of crimson and white.

The Care and Feeding of Your Aries Marriage

THE PURPOSE OF AN ARIES MARRIAGE

The marriage begun with the Sun in Aries has an evolutionary imperative to **lead**, and as a team you're always at your best when you're blazing new trails. Your union sometimes makes you capable of doing things that other people don't, can't, or won't do. You'll be the first among your friends to have children, or to declare you're not having them at all. You'll forcefully exert your independent streak by moving far from everyone you know, keeping a healthy distance from your families, and making a whole new batch of friends.

WHAT THE ARIES MARRIAGE NEEDS

In order to really be yourselves and to build a life that is not just about trying something new for the sake of novelty, you need a challenge that will captivate you both. You are likely to find success by recognizing opportunities and seizing them, adding value, and then passing them on to others who are more interested in managing them day to day. You have a knack for recognizing hidden potential, so you might do well in purchasing or building a business or a property, improving or refurbishing it, and reselling later at a profit.

SOURCES OF FRICTION

In his classic film *Annie Hall*, Woody Allen muses that "A relationship is like a shark. It has to constantly move forward or it dies." This may be especially true of the Aries marriage, and the drive to constantly keep moving forward can mean you don't always have enough patience to ride out the rough spots in your marriage. The same determination that serves you so well when you're working together toward a goal can make you ferocious adversaries when you find yourselves on opposite sides of an argument. Fortunately, the friction that builds up between you can usually be easily diffused through strenuous exercise or—happily!—sex.

The Aries Marriage Style

THE FACE YOU SHOW THE WORLD

From the outside, the Aries marriage looks absolutely ideal, a fairy tale come to life. You appear affectionate yet independent, with a no-nonsense approach to any situation. As a team, you seem blessed with an unshakable confidence that allows you to move through life unfettered by self-doubt. It's this apparent confidence and vision that inspires others to follow your lead.

WHAT YOU OWN

You really enjoy money. You like everything about it. It's not unusual for you to collect actual, tangible money, such as interesting currency from other lands or old coins. Your thinking about financial matters is that you should enjoy what you have—not that you should be profligate in your spending, or excessively ambitious about earning money, but that the things you own and the way you spend your money should bring pleasure and stability to you and to those you love.

You are quite adept at handling money, and one or the other of you can usually be found working in banking, real estate, financial planning, accounting, appraisal, or interior design. Your appreciation for material resources extends to other parts of the physical world too, and you're likely to enjoy outdoor activities that include hunting, fishing, or gathering.

HOW YOU COMMUNICATE

You adore chatting with one another, and your love of language is contagious. You love running errands around your neighborhood, make a point of learning the names of your postal carrier and the checker at the local produce market, and never forget to send greeting cards for Christmas, birthdays, births, deaths, and wedding anniversaries.

You're talented networkers, and almost never have to rely on the yellow pages or classified ads to find what you need. Whether you're looking for a job, a car, or a sofa, you almost certainly know someone among your network of friends, family, co-workers, neighbors, and other social circles who can help you find it—and you're more than happy to return the favor. Second only to the Gemini marriage, you're a terrific resource for connecting people with other people, things, and opportunities.

HOW YOU LIVE

You may be constantly on the go, but when you do land at home you fully inhabit your environment. Your home is cozy, lived-in, and well stocked with good food, and there are nearly always "strays" at your dinner table. Your hospitality and warmth magnetize your overworked business associates, friends from church, neighbor kids—and all are made to feel welcome and well fed.

You are trailblazers in other areas of life, but your home tends to be rather traditional. Both of you are fond of doing things the way you saw them done in your own families. In fact, this is an area of likely conflict between you: the battle for supremacy over whose family traditions will be observed. Make a conscious effort to develop new traditions that are unique to *your* family, while including nostalgic touches from your individual upbringings.

YOUR CHILDREN AND CREATIVE SPIRIT

You are wonderful parents, because you haven't forgotten what it's like to be children yourselves. You encourage your children to have fun and to pursue (and to stick with) meaningful hobbies, and your support nurtures their confidence and happiness. Consequently, your children tend to be creative, expressive, generous, and warm-hearted.

You're a romantic couple, the type to set aside time for "dates" with each other. You continue the romantic rituals of courtship—gift-giving, affectionate nicknames, hand-holding—well into your married life. Romance is particularly important to your sense of yourselves as a couple, so give this side of your relationship all the creative energy you can muster.

YOUR WORK, HEALTH, AND DAILY ROUTINE

You're happiest in jobs that allow you plenty of control over both the quality of your work and the level of service you can provide. Your standards and work ethics are demanding, and you generally dislike taking direction from others. Regardless of your professions, it's important to both of you that you are able to take a hands-on approach to your work. At the end of each work day, you like to be able to point to tangible results—a stack of paper, a pile of envelopes, a product that has been created—that represent your labors. You would not be particularly satisfied in management jobs, overseeing the labors of others, though you are happy enough to create new opportunities for others to use their gifts and skills.

You tend to burn the midnight oil and to worry a bit too much, especially about your work, and so you need to promote a lifestyle in your home that supports relaxation. Otherwise, you may create a lifestyle that is stressful and does not support robust health. This is easily avoided; reasonable standards of cleanliness and efficiency combined with sane schedules are all that is needed to keep your daily lives running smoothly.

YOUR FRIENDS AND FOES

As a couple, you favor direct and uncomplicated dealings with the world, its people, and its challenges. As long as you interact with like-minded souls, all is well; but your directness can, from time to time, put you on a collision course with those who prefer a more tactful approach. If these people are your friends and have your best interests at heart, they can show you ways to curb your tendency toward tactlessness and to practice more diplomatic and collaborative approaches to handling disagreements.

Your direct approach has its strengths too, and you are particularly adept at helping the people closest to you make tough decisions and confront difficult situations. Some who might benefit from your example choose to ignore it, and to use their negative qualities against you. They do so at their peril, because like Mars, the patron god of your marriage, you are ruthless opponents when someone makes war with you.

WHAT YOU SHARE

Though you are generally straightforward and even naïvely candid about nearly everything else, you are rather secretive about two things: your sex life and your net worth. You feel it is disloyal to talk to others about the most intimate pleasures of your marriage, and indiscreet—even foolhardy—to let others know the extent of your riches. You are, however, deeply moved by those who are in pain, disabled, or truly weak and defenseless, and with them you are exceedingly generous in sharing what you have.

Generally speaking, your sex life is excellent—unless there has been a breach of trust between you, particularly infidelity or financial misconduct. Otherwise, you enjoy enviable emotional and physical intimacy and good luck with shared resources such as investments or even inheritance.

WHAT YOU BELIEVE

You encourage one another to take risks—to expand your boundaries of consciousness, especially by traveling to new places and experiencing different ways of life. In fact, you are reluctant to discourage or limit one another in any way; this is a wonderfully validating attitude, but of course this kind of unconditional support can actually be harmful when one of you is headed in the wrong direction. Misguided or self-destructive impulses are best checked and constrained by those who know and love you best, and you should be able to look to one another for that kind of reality check.

You may or may not be religious people in the strictest sense of the word; it's important to both of you, however, to share a common philosophy toward life that can serve as your guide and inspiration. It may be a philosophy as simple as "Everyone should be free to do his or her own thing" or "An unexamined life is not worth living" or even "Tomorrow is another day." Cultivating this sense of your place in the grand scheme of things is key to retaining a sense of joyousness and optimism in your marriage.

YOUR CONTRIBUTION TO THE WORLD

You are exceptionally well equipped for self-employment, because although you may be a bit hasty about entering into new situations, once you are involved in an enterprise you are excellent strategists. As a team, you're exceptionally good at setting long-range goals and systematically pursuing them. You have your own ideas about how things should be done, and you find that few people match your drive and vision. So, you set out early in your marriage to either support each other in self-employment or, ideally, build a business operation together.

If you do work for others, you will fare happiest in careers that allow you to be in charge, or careers that involve challenge, competition, or even combat (such as the military, sports, or certain kinds of law). Aries also favors professions that involve working with metal, blades, or heat, such as surgeons, blacksmiths, butchers, or barbers. Regardless of the work you choose, your marriage will help propel you both into positions of leadership and authority.

YOUR PLACE IN SOCIETY

As a couple, you form friendships and social connections that are stable and enduring, if not particularly intimate or emotional. You yourselves tend to have a difficult time fitting in with other people, because most of them simply can't keep up with you! Likewise, your friends and associates generally have some quality of strangeness about them. Groups of astrologers, science fiction aficionados, fringe religious groups, beatniks, and anarchists—you are all drawn together by what makes you different from the rest of society rather than what makes you alike.

You will likely retain your vigor into late life, and in fact will improve with age. You will be the sort of couple whom younger people seek out because your wit, vitality, and continued interest in life are inspiring. At all stages of your marriage, you magnetize friends of all ages, often from backgrounds that are very different from your own. Because you have both had the experience of being outsiders, you make a special effort to make everyone around you feel accepted and welcome.

YOUR PRIVATE SANCTUARY

You share a profound sense of vulnerability, which you take great care to hide from the rest of the world. You are much given to charitable acts behind the scenes and spiritual exploration, and when no one is looking, you even cry at sad movies.

You fear aging more than most couples, because you're afraid of becoming ill and weak. Let that fear motivate you to take care of your health and provide financially for your old age. Even when you're young, though, you are a little afraid of that part of you that has doubts, that can see all points of view and shades of gray. Self-doubt is the greatest potential enemy of your marriage—but it will only defeat you if you deny your insecurities rather than acknowledging and bravely overcoming them. Courage, after all, isn't the absence of fear but the overcoming of it—and courage is the defining motif of your entire marriage.

The Taurus Marriage

(APRIL 21–MAY 21)

Famous Sun-in-Taurus Marriages

Queen Elizabeth and King George VI (April 26)
Arnold Schwarzenegger and Maria Shriver (April 26)
Tom Hanks and Rita Wilson (April 30)
Tipper and Al Gore (May 19)

❧

After her mother died, Margaret became her clan's *de facto materfamilias*. Family holidays automatically migrated to her home. She became the hub of communication, fielding bulletins from far-flung family members about births, deaths, marriages, moves, and job changes. It's a role she never particularly craved—she's an independent Aquarius—but in the end, she was swept into it by the tide of popular opinion.

That, and the powerful magnetism of her Taurus marriage to Sam. Theirs is a happy compatibility: Margaret is energetic and determinedly upbeat, Sam is cheerful and outgoing. Within a couple of years of their lovely, traditional wedding ceremony, they bought a house and welcomed their first child. They worked in steady, dependable jobs, were active in their church, sent out their Christmas cards on time, and were thoroughly nice people.

They still are . . . and aside from a second child and a larger house, their lives don't look appreciably different than they did twenty years ago. Mind you, this is not meant as a criticism; several generations of family members *depend* on that marriage. Because of Margaret and her husband, brothers and sisters, nephews and cousins all know where they'll be eating turkey each Thanksgiving, and they know there will be plenty of delicious side dishes to go along with it. They know where to get a distant cousin's e-mail address, or to find out the name of their great-grandmother.

The Taurus marriage is, above all, *stable*. It is as comforting and unchanging as going home to Mom and Dad's house for the holidays. Even among the rich and famous, Taurus marriages stand out as among the most enduring: good-guy Tom Hanks and his wife, Rita Wilson; the Queen Mum and her King George; Al and Tipper. These are not flashy, headline-making marriages—rather, they are marriages that testify to the worth and endurance of the institution itself.

The Taurus Season

The Sun is in Taurus from late April through the first few weeks of May, when spring is in lush, riotous bloom. Roses are heavy and fragrant, the sun is warm, the air still has a tender tang. Sensuous and delicious as ripe fruit, it's one of the most beautiful seasons in which to marry. Is it any wonder that a season so full of bounty, beauty, and lovely weather breeds marriages that are prosperous and contented?

The month may have been named for the goddess Maia, the Greek counterpart of Bona Dea, the Roman goddess of fertility. May 1 is May Day, a celebration of winter's end that derives from the pagan festival of Beltane. In many parts of Europe, May Day is still celebrated with community festivals and the Maypole dance, honoring spring as a season of fertility.

In astrology, Taurus is ruled by Venus, the goddess of beauty and delight, a rulership it shares with Libra. Whereas Libra reflects Venus's principle of relationship, Taurus emphasizes the Venusian enjoyment of the physical world and its bounty. Those born under the sign of the bull are solid, stable, and enjoy simple pleasures, but they can also be stubborn and dangerous when provoked. This is the shadow side of the Taurus marriage: the danger of becoming stuck and self-satisfied, and of falling so much in love with what you have that you are over-protective of it.

How It Begins: The Taurus Wedding

Traditional, family-oriented, not particularly flashy, the Taurus wedding has a sweet, old-fashioned charm. Taurus, ruled by sensual Venus, enjoys luxury as much as anyone, but cherishes practicality above all else and is embarrassed by fuss. A simple ceremony, followed by a buffet reception with delicious food and a tasty cake, suits you just fine. The weather is usually perfect, and Taurus, along with Virgo and Sagittarius, is particularly fond of nature—so celebrate outdoors if you can.

Music will be carefully chosen to be as unobtrusive as possible, and will lean toward traditional choices. You are somewhat less likely than other couples to write your own wedding vows, preferring to keep your private sentiments to yourselves.

Taurus favors soft pastel colors, particularly pink and baby blue, which is a bit surprising given Taurus's fondness for practicality and earthiness. My Taurus mother, who was decidedly down-to-earth, never failed to surprise me with her love of pink. Her entire bedroom was pink, from the pink carpet to the pink flowers on her bedspread. And she loved ruffles. (Brides of the Taurus season: when choosing colors and styles for your bridesmaids' dresses, please take it easy with the pink, baby blue, and ruffles. Your sportier bridesmaids will thank you!)

Fill your day with flowers: flowers for bouquets, centerpieces, and headpieces; flowers for the church, and for the top of the cake. Nothing honors Taurus more than filling your wedding day with the Earth's lavish beauty. For your Taurus wedding, you can't go wrong with roses, which are in season now and available in every imaginable color. Mix in a bit of lily of the valley and hawthorn, two other flowers associated with Taurus. If you're on a limited budget, locate a farmer's market or wholesale flower mart that will be open the day of your wedding and arrange for a friend to pay a visit and load up on the prettiest and freshest blooms on the morning of your ceremony.

The Care and Feeding of Your Taurus Marriage

THE PURPOSE OF A TAURUS MARRIAGE

Your Taurus marriage is at its best and happiest when it provides a source of **security**, **sustenance**, and **stability**—for the bridal couple, but also for friends, family, children, and neighbors. Taurus enjoys life and its many pleasures in a quiet, contented, uncomplicated way. As a couple, you tend to take things as they come and don't overanalyze. A church wedding and buffet reception, a house in the suburbs, and two kids worked fine for Mom and Dad; why rock the boat?

You may look at your friends and siblings in their intense Scorpionic or restless Gemini marriages and wonder what in the world they're looking for. Why are they so dissatisfied, so seemingly intent on thinking and talking and probing all the simple enjoyment out of life? And why do they always bring those weird, exotic side dishes for Thanksgiving dinner—what's wrong with good old mashed potatoes the way Mom made them? Why do we need garlic in there?

Possessing the gravitational pull of the Earth itself, your marriage is the fixed center of your family, friends, and community, lending practical advice, money, and a hearty Sunday dinner to those who are in need or in flux.

WHAT THE TAURUS MARRIAGE NEEDS

Security. Routine. Real estate. Creature comforts. Community. You've entered marriage for the long haul. In other areas of your lives you may be driven, ambitious, or restless, but you count on your marriage to furnish a stable platform from which to launch worldly success.

Taurus savors tangible symbols of security and success, so in order to feel you are on the right track, you need money—enough to be able to spend some, save some, and invest some. You need well-paying jobs, a comfortable home, good friends, and an overall sense of peace, plenty, and predictability. Your needs are simple, and having fulfilled them, you are content to relax and leave the striving to more ambitious signs.

For tortured, dramatic, driven, or unorthodox souls, **the stability of the Taurus marriage can feel stifling.** In the same way we grow impatient with our reliable, dependable parents once we're old enough to seek our independence, you may occasionally find yourselves a bit bored by the very stability that you value in your marriage. The antidote for dullness is a healthy dose of passion, drama, and unpredictability. No one is suggesting you give up your Friday night pizza-and-movie dates altogether in favor of tango dancing, nightclub hopping, and orgies. But it wouldn't kill you to try a new restaurant once in a while or go to the theater—and you need to make a conscious effort to keep the intimate side of your marriage interesting too.

The Taurus Marriage Style

THE FACE YOU SHOW THE WORLD

"Slow and steady" is your marriage mantra. You're a not a couple that can be pressured into acting on anything before you're ready; even if you don't have any particular reservations, you'll drag your heels just to make sure you're not overlooking any potential problems. Once you've made up your mind to commit to a course of action, though, dynamite couldn't blast you off course.

WHAT YOU OWN

As mentioned, Taurus has an affinity for money, and it is an interest that transcends mere avarice. You are intellectually challenged and fascinated by the subject of money. You enjoy talking about money and playing with spreadsheets that show you how much you're worth, and you have a lot of ideas about how to earn it, keep it, and spend it. You like to think you're financially prudent, but although you move deliberately—especially in making major purchases—you're quite capable of justifying a dubious purchase because it's "practical" or "a good investment."

Fortunately, the two of you don't usually find it difficult to earn money. Generally you have multiple income streams and a healthy sense of your worth in the marketplace. You're always thinking of new ways to use your capital to create more wealth and are ever-so-slightly susceptible to "get rich quick" schemes, especially those delivered at a lightning-fast pace and with an appeal to "logic."

HOW YOU COMMUNICATE

If there is one area where you're given to sentimentality, it's in the way you communicate with one another. Baby talk, pet names, and terms of endearment pepper your conversations with each other; it's amazing how often Taurus marriage couples refer to each other as "mama" and "papa." You find it very upsetting to argue or disagree with each other, and may use food as a way to calm yourselves down or to say "I'm sorry."

Your home, like Margaret's, will likely become a second home for your siblings and your neighbors, and they'll think nothing of dropping by and rummaging through your refrigerator. Mostly you don't mind—you've got plenty to go around—but on occasion you can resent sharing, feeling it detracts from your security and well-being. There's nothing wrong with setting appropriate boundaries about how much you share with others, as long as you keep in mind that sharing can be an important way of enjoying what you have.

HOW YOU LIVE

You enjoy life's creature comforts, and nowhere is this more apparent than in your home. This is where you really lash out and spend money on the latest toys, gadgets, and entertainment equipment. You entertain often, and you want your guests to be impressed by your home and belongings. If you have children, your home is probably the most popular gathering place for the neighborhood's children because there are always good things to eat and new toys to play with.

Your taste for luxury emerges at home too, and little expense is spared on comfortable furniture, good linens, and fine fixtures. While your impulse is to purchase only the finest quality goods, bear in mind that you enjoy updating your home's "fashions" on a regular basis, so you may not actually need to spend a lot of money on, say, linens that are made to last for fifty years.

YOUR CHILDREN AND CREATIVE SPIRIT

Your children will be taught their manners, be expected to pick up after themselves, and be trained to floss their teeth and care for their belongings. Teach them practical life skills too, like balancing a checkbook, changing the oil in a car, and upgrading the components on their computers. Be cautious, though, about becoming too critical about occasional lapses in grammar and spelling or didactic about homework, scheduling, and rules. It's your job to enforce good habits, but the effective parent knows when to cut a kid a little slack. Focus on teaching critical thinking so your children are able to monitor their own behavior and set their own schedules.

Your marriage encourages practicality, so your creative impulses are likely to be diverted into producing useful objects. A love of woodworking will be channeled into creating beautiful, well-used pieces of furniture; knitting, needlework, and quilting will produce clothing and blankets that provide warmth and comfort. You prefer hobbies that occupy your hands, including playing musical instruments, along with woodworking, needlework, stained glass, or gardening.

YOUR WORK, HEALTH, AND DAILY ROUTINE

You like a harmonious daily routine with few ups and downs, but you're prone to stresses that knock your work/life balance out of whack. You are susceptible to diseases caused by overindulgence in rich food and drink and a general disinclination toward exercise. That said, marriage is generally very good for your health, because it encourages a regular, balanced schedule and offers a built-in support system. It's especially good for you if your partner uses his or her considerable influence to help you to cultivate good habits, such as exercise and a healthy diet.

You enjoy pets but decry the messes they create, especially damage to carpets, upholstery, and woodwork. When selecting pets, choose those that are naturally fastidious and learn in advance how they may be trained not to damage property. Also, take your lifestyles carefully into account, and don't choose animals that need more companionship than you are able to give.

YOUR FRIENDS AND FOES

You prefer to enjoy life and take things as they come. Perhaps because you are so solid and easy-going, you magnetize people who are dramatic and intense, and who dwell on the dark side of life. These people can have an interesting and healthy influence on your marriage, prompting you to give thought and attention to matters that are important and challenging.

If you find, though, that you consistently attract people who are too intense for comfort, or who seem to rely on you a bit too much, consider the possibility that such people may reflect parts of your marriage that are being repressed. Challenge yourselves to acknowledge the ugly and imperfect parts of life, instead of stubbornly insisting that everything is perfectly fine, and you will be less apt to attract people who seem determined to make you confront those things.

WHAT YOU SHARE

My no-nonsense Taurus mother was fond of saying, "You don't talk about sex . . . you *do* it." The Taurus marriage encourages sensuality and a healthy appreciation for sexual expression, but prefers that it be fun, uncomplicated, and largely unspoken of. Religious or other belief systems likely have a strong influence on this area of your life as well, and may dictate your approach to sexual expression and practical matters such as contraception.

Shared resources are another area in which couples blend in an intimate way, and you tend to have a fairly trusting, optimistic approach to your finances. You are interested in money—especially in ways to earn it and spend it—but abstractions such as investments, insurance, and 401k plans hold little fascination for you. You're much more interested in what you have right now. Creating tangible representations of your investments, such as flow charts and diagrams, will help make the subject somewhat more compelling.

WHAT YOU BELIEVE

Rules are extremely important to you, and your ethics tend to be drawn in black and white. Your philosophies and politics lean toward the conservative, and you are likely to either reject religious doctrine completely or to almost zealously embrace organized religion—often of a very restrictive variety.

If you travel, it's generally for work or to enjoy the kind of vacations you remember from your youth. Even if you were both globetrotting bohemians before marriage, you may find within a few years of your wedding that you're grumbling about taxes, welfare, and "foreigners." Limiting and containing that which is unfamiliar tends to be a requirement for living the stable, secure lifestyle that you desire.

YOUR CONTRIBUTION TO THE WORLD

You would really prefer to own a business together, or two businesses of your own, because you dislike being forced into rigid schedules. You like to work at your own pace and organize things in your own way. You crave stability in most areas of life, but in your careers you thrive on excitement and unpredictability. Working as consultants, or in careers that are paid on a bonus or commission basis, is an exciting challenge for you.

You may work with your friends, or make many friends through your work, and you may be involved in media, broadcasting, sales, politics, or technology. You're always involved with ideas and technologies that are ahead of the curve, sensing trends well ahead of the general public; the challenge lies in presenting your revolutionary visions in a way that is palatable and useful to people who are slow to adapt.

YOUR PLACE IN SOCIETY

You're not inclined to draft long-term plans, preferring to let the future take care of itself—and generally speaking, it does. Your friends tend to be people who share your spiritual beliefs. Often there is a caretaking bond between you and your friends; because your lives are well structured and rather predictable, you enjoy friends who live casual, fluid lives, even if they are somewhat chaotic and disorganized. This is fine as far as it goes, but charity alone is not a solid basis for a real friendship between equals. Be careful to cultivate friends who are fun, imaginative, and creative, but who are also responsible.

You are fairly conservative about many things, but curiously resistant to planning for your retirement and old age. Unless you are fortunate enough to possess a huge trust fund, a close family, perfect health, and many compelling interests, this is a part of life you can't afford to ignore. It can, in fact, be the most spiritually rich and creative time of both your lives.

YOUR PRIVATE SANCTUARY

You probably disagree more than anyone realizes, but you feel it's important to keep your arguments private. You are also more ambitious than you appear on the surface, and a bit more ruthless about getting what you want—which poses certain difficulties, because you feel uncomfortable expressing these ambitions openly. If you find yourselves condemning others as selfish, it's a signal that the two of you may be suppressing your own ambitions too harshly. There's nothing inherently wrong with wanting to get ahead; it's only wrong if you hurt others along the way.

Though it's not usually the first thing that people notice about you, you are in fact passionate advocates on a wide range of issues. Because you appear placid and cheerful on the surface, the intensity of your convictions and your willingness to fight for what you believe in often takes people by surprise. You are wonderful champions of the underdog—and formidable opponents when you're crossed!

The Gemini Marriage
(MAY 22–JUNE 21)

Famous Sun-in-Gemini Marriages

The Duke and Duchess of Windsor (June 3)
Bruce Springsteen and Patti Scialfa (June 8)
Sylvia Plath and Ted Hughes (June 16)
Martin Luther King Jr. and Coretta Scott (June 18)

✦✦✦

At a pivotal moment in the film *L.A. Story*, Steve Martin finds himself trapped in an elegant but deadly dull dinner party. Fortunately he's accompanied by a captivating English journalist, a woman he has gently pursued for some time. During an especially dreary speech, they absent themselves from the party for a stroll through a beautiful garden. There they quickly find themselves overtaken by passion, engaging in their first intimate encounter. Later that evening, as they drift along Melrose Boulevard hand-in-hand, they peer wide-eyed into store windows and gaze at ordinary people and objects around them as if seeing them for the first time. The camera pans away for a moment, and when it settles again on Martin and his love they are portrayed by two child actors in oversized formal clothing, looking dazzled and happy.

And that, I think, is my favorite image of the Gemini marriage: at its best, it's a union of dazzled, happy children in grown-up clothing. As the two of you stroll through life, hand-in-hand, you behold your world with the shining, curious gaze of the young. Everything is new, everything is interesting—and you always have a willing accomplice when you need to escape a dull dinner party.

The Gemini Season

The Sun is in Gemini from late May through the first few weeks of June, arguably the most popular time of year for weddings. When I dreamed of weddings as a young girl, though—which, admittedly, was not often—I always pictured myself getting married in October. Brightly colored leaves combined with sunshine and crisp air—what's not to love? As it turned out, my husband and I, after getting engaged in February, simply couldn't wait until October, so we married on a sweltering-hot Memorial Day Sunday. Although an unconventional couple in many ways, we had somehow joined the legions of bridal couples who walk down the aisle in June and late May, while the Sun is in Gemini.

June, when the Sun is in Gemini for most of the month, has such a long tradition of popularity for weddings that it even takes its name from Juno, the Roman goddess of marriage. There are plenty of good reasons for June's popularity among bridal couples, the most obvious being the return of warm, sunny weather in most parts of the Northern Hemisphere. Many prospective couples wish to marry *al fresco*, but even those who hold their ceremony indoors don't want to have to slog through mud and rain on their way to the church.

On a more practical note, in the days before birth control and premarital sex, marrying in June meant hopefully conceiving a child in time to give birth the next spring and recover before harvest. This was obviously an advantage in agrarian societies where every pair of hands was needed.

Astrologically, however, June is a curious choice for marriage. The Sun in Gemini has a reputation for quickness and cleverness, but not constancy. Gemini is childlike, mischievous, and androgynous; these are not qualities that spring to mind when we think of a bride and groom. Gemini brings valuable traits to the altar too, of course: flexibility, a love of laughter, and a genuine interest in most everything. In particular, Gemini has a passion for what experts agree is the single most important skill in a successful marriage: communication.

How It Begins: The Gemini Wedding

Mischievous, witty, and clever, Gemini has charm to spare, and your wedding and reception will be the best party of the summer. Your single friends will meet and mingle, the married folks will renew old acquaintances, the kids will make new friends—and everyone will have a fantastic time.

Gemini is a fabulous sign for parties, and the reception promises sparkling conversation, shameless flirtation, and enough scandalous behavior to keep gossips happy for months to come. Gemini enjoys variety and prefers to mingle while dining, so a buffet-style reception is a better choice than a sit-down dinner. And offer guests those bubble-wand party favors, perfect for christening the bridal couple as they leave for their honeymoon. Gemini adores bubbles, balloons, and anything else that floats through the air.

Gemini is associated with the colors yellow and light blue, the colors of the late spring sky. But remember: Gemini likes variety, and that extends to colors! Take an eclectic, patchwork-quilt approach to the colors for your wedding. Let your bridesmaids choose gowns in complementary, rather than matching, colors.

Roses are a popular choice of flowers for May and June weddings because they are in season and available in a wide variety of colors, but personally, I consider the lush, sensual quality of the rose a better choice for an early-May, Taurus wedding. If you want to use roses—and who wouldn't?—choose yellow and white ones and pair them with something unexpected, like peonies or ranunculus. Honor the curious, witty spirit of Gemini with flowers of interesting shapes, like lily of the valley, stargazer lily, or even bells of Ireland.

But what about after you walk down the aisle? After the bubbles have dissolved and the peonies have wilted, what kind of marriage will you have on your hands?

The Care and Feeding of Your Gemini Marriage

THE PURPOSE OF A GEMINI MARRIAGE

The curiosity and sociability of your Gemini marriage make you a natural networking unit—a source for **connections** of all kinds. If one of your friends needs a plumber, you'll have a phone number to give her. When your brother is looking for a partner to accompany him on his Monday morning hikes, you immediately suggest two or three potential candidates. Guests come to a party at your house and leave with two or three new friends, a couple of business cards, and a recipe for a terrific bean dip. Gemini's rallying cry is, "I know a guy ..."—a guy who can give you a deal on a car, the perfect tile for your kitchen floor, or a date to remember.

You meet new people everywhere. Whatever your individual personalities, you tend to be a pretty friendly couple, whether chatting with strangers in line at the supermarket or asking your pest control guy how his kids are adjusting to school. And so you build connections, until your Gemini marriage has become mission control, smack in the middle of a web of acquaintances, information, and ideas that keeps your circle of friends moving.

WHAT THE GEMINI MARRIAGE NEEDS

Gemini has a bit of a flighty reputation and is often accused of being fickle or dishonest. Does this mean the Gemini marriage is doomed to infidelity and dishonesty? No; it's much closer to the truth to say that Gemini needs a **constant variety** of sounds, sights, and ideas in order to remain vibrant and to feel alive. The real reason a Gemini marriage might fail is that the two people in it stop talking to each other or become too rigid in their points of view. Gemini embraces astrologer Caroline Casey's mantra: *Believe nothing; entertain possibilities*.

Gemini marriages stand or fall on the strength of **communication**. If you're a couple who loves to talk, especially to each other, the Gemini marriage will suit you down to the ground. At the very least, you'll never become one of those sad-looking couples sitting across from each other in a café with nothing to talk about!

SOURCES OF FRICTION

The same needs that feed and sustain the Gemini marriage may, of course, grow tiresome if yours is a very different kind of personality. Are you a loner? Do you need lots of peace, quiet, and routine to refuel your energy? Do you hate gossip and small talk? The Gemini marriage will have moments that try your soul. There is so much motion, background noise, and light social interaction in your day-to-day lives together that finding quiet, private moments may be a challenge!

Even if you are a social, convivial sort, you'll need to find a balance in your daily life between the desire for constant stimulation and a sane, human need for occasional peace and quiet. A room or corner in your home dedicated to reflection and contemplation, one weekend a month with no social commitments, an occasional afternoon nap—all are ways of quieting Gemini's mental energy and nourishing the other, more intuitive qualities of your marriage.

The Gemini Marriage Style

THE FACE YOU SHOW THE WORLD

The Gemini marriage approaches each new situation as an opportunity to meet someone or learn something new. You enjoy social interactions that arise organically, such as chatting with a neighbor over the fence or running errands with a friend, and you're loath to accept formal invitations because you don't like to be pinned down to a schedule. You tend to be a popular couple all the same, for everything from casual gatherings to formal parties, because you more than keep up your end of the conversation. In fact, you prefer to ask other people questions about their lives than volunteer details about your own!

WHAT YOU OWN

If there is one subject sure to elicit strong feelings from the normally breezy Gemini couple, it's money. This couple, more than most, equates money with security, and also with caring. You are likely to invest in real estate and relatively conservative securities. However, though you may be conservative in your investments, you are generous with loved ones, sharing money, resources, and hospitality. You put a lot of thought into gift giving, both with each other and with the people you care about. But because the face you present to the world is light and casual, few of your family and friends realize just how hurt you can feel when your generosity is not appreciated or reciprocated.

HOW YOU COMMUNICATE

The Gemini couple loves to talk, and prefers the sound of each other's voices to any music. You adore exchanging ideas with others too, and your favorite way to spend an evening is to host a lively dinner party and invite all your wittiest friends for great conversation. You excel at tag-team storytelling and are not averse to bending the truth a little bit to improve a story. You are also natural teachers and writers, with a real flair for presenting facts with drama and passion.

If you have children, their upbringing will emphasize good grammar and poised self-expression; they will learn early on that they can get away with just about anything as long as they are able to manufacture a defense or excuse that will entertain you!

HOW YOU LIVE

Your home is not necessarily tidy, but tends to have the simple charm of the utilitarian. There are few purely ornamental baubles and knick-knacks; you prefer good-quality, sturdy furnishings that are designed for service and utility. Almost always, home is also a workplace for at least one of you, so a comfortable, well-appointed home office is a must. You tend to be sensitive to sounds, so if you live in an urban environment you will need to devise some kind of screening or soundproofing against unwelcome noise.

You are more likely to visit your families in their homes rather than entertain them in yours. In fact, as much as you enjoy extending hospitality, you're actually uncomfortable when guests come to stay for more than a few days. You are creatures of very specific habit and dislike interruptions in your daily routine.

YOUR CHILDREN AND CREATIVE SPIRIT

You encourage the children in your lives to cultivate beauty, artistry, musical ability, and charm. The result can be truly lovely children, or smarmy, unctuous Eddie Haskell clones. The key lies in encouraging inner harmony and a genuine desire to get along with others, rather than simply the outward appearance of these traits.

But the Gemini couple is more likely than some to forego having children of their own in favor of following an artistic muse. Money and attention that might have been lavished on offspring are diverted instead to creative projects, hobbies, and each other. The Gemini couple is unusually versatile and creative, with many interests and activities, and might prefer to devote energy to these interests rather than raising children. In many ways, you feel like children yourselves.

YOUR WORK, HEALTH, AND DAILY ROUTINE

You are an intense couple when it comes to work matters. Workaholics, even. Once you become embroiled in a job or a project, you are completely immersed; like pit bulls, you stay on task until the project is finished! You may also find that, as a couple, you have a natural ability to rehabilitate and restore things; in combination with your acumen for investing in real estate, you may do very well by purchasing properties, fixing them up, and reselling them.

Generally, you will likely feel happiest when you are able to work for yourselves. When it comes to work, you like feeling in control of your own destinies, and you vehemently dislike being told what to do and having someone else schedule your work for you!

YOUR FRIENDS AND FOES

Gemini likes to take a freewheeling, noncommittal approach to life, entertaining a variety of ideas, moving fluidly through a variety of situations, settings, and relationships. The people you draw into your inner circle tend to enlarge your perspective: people who are passionately committed to causes and ideals, who don't hesitate to become involved in the lives of others, and who always have their eye on the big picture. In turn, you offer fresh perspectives and new ideas.

As a couple, you are most likely to find friends through your activities and interests in education, publishing, and travel. These are also the areas of life where you tend to run into conflicts—often of a religious, political, or philosophical nature—with people who take a fundamentally different view of life than you do.

WHAT YOU SHARE

Sex is rarely the basis of a Gemini marriage. It's not that you *mind* sex, of course; it's just that other concerns—say, good conversation, or work—tend to take priority. Your sex life tends to work best when it's scheduled. Spontaneity may rule the day in other parts of your relationship, but sex—while you certainly enjoy it while it's happening!—practically needs to be put on your calendar before you'll pay attention to it.

Your shared financial picture tends to be rosiest when one or the other of you is placed explicitly in charge. Schedule regular "business meetings" to discuss budget and long-term financial strategies and goals, but leave the day-to-day bill paying to just one of you. Often the Gemini marriage will employ professionals to consult with them about specific aspects of their joint finances—you almost certainly have a tax accountant or investment manager on staff—but Gemini is protective about money, so no one gets a blank check with your signatures on it.

WHAT YOU BELIEVE

Religion, travel, and higher education are all closely connected with our beliefs about the world. If you're in a Gemini marriage, you may find that while you are both well known around your neighborhood, your community, and your city, you find it a bit challenging to venture very far from your familiar surroundings. Now, before you pick up that pen to write me a long letter about your Gemini marriage and your passports filled with stamps from many continents, wait for the disclaimer: if you both love to travel, and your individual birth charts clearly point to loads of adventures over both land and sea, well, marrying with the Sun in Gemini is probably not going to curtail that.

The Gemini marriage is generally more interested in exploring religious ideas than pledging allegiance to a particular denomination, and happier pursuing short-term classes to learn practical skills than advanced degrees in weighty subjects. You are somewhat more apt to get involved with churches that advance humanitarian and egalitarian goals, or to pursue higher education in the sciences or technology. But your progress will tend to be of the start-and-stop variety, so online, home study, or other flexible education programs work best for you.

YOUR CONTRIBUTION TO THE WORLD

Before you were married, you may have been real go-getters in the business areas of your lives. Once you got married, though, this part of your lives became a little more muddled. You began to enjoy hanging out and chatting together rather than working until all hours. You began to question the long-term wisdom of a career path that serves only materialistic and not spiritual goals. In short, you became . . . if not exactly slackers, at least more sympathetic to the slacker philosophy of hanging loose and living on little.

Should you long for more tangible, worldly success, the key lies in including fun and spiritual objectives as part of your career game plan. Having a noble goal in mind, such as early retirement in order to have more time for good works, can make it easier for you to focus on what you need to do to get from here to there.

Part of the problem is that you may not have good examples of parents or other influential people in your lives who had careers that seemed like they were *intentional*, rather than accidental. Hopefully, as you align your career paths with a spiritual purpose, you will attract mentors to inspire you on your journey. In turn, you can become mentors to a new generation.

YOUR PLACE IN SOCIETY

Your natural friends and allies tend to be lone wolves, entrepreneurs, and explorers. As a result, you will rarely find yourselves part of a "group" of friends unless you are in a leadership role. Among your friends, you will likely be the ones who organize parties, outings, and other social events that bring everyone together. This might be an area of tension between the two of you. How much work should be put into these activities? Whom should you invite?

You envision a future in which you are independent, cantankerous old people living in a wild frontier setting, depending on no one and making do for yourselves. One of your great horrors is the thought of spending your final years in a nursing home or communal living situation, or indeed to be dependent on others for anything. With this in mind, live your life in the present with a view to remaining as physically and financially fit as possible, so you are less likely to become disabled or destitute in your old age.

YOUR PRIVATE SANCTUARY

Because you're chatty and funny and interested in a lot of different things, people tend to think that you never just spend an evening vegging out in front of the TV with a bowl of popcorn.

How wrong they are.

The secret life of the Gemini marriage is a life of comfort, hedonism, and a preoccupation with tasty food and drink. Soft sheets. Plush sofas. What most people don't know about the two of you is just how acquisitive you can be! You want the good life of fine wine, evenings at the theater, and country vacation homes. Oh, maybe not to the exclusion of such intangibles as good conversation and personal freedom, but certainly more than your breezy exterior might suggest.

You're also a lot more secure and staid than most people think you are. You seem changeable, even flighty, with a limitless fount of new ideas and gentle fantasies about a future doing good works for the needy. But you've almost always got a stash of money put aside against hard times. You've almost always got a comfy home that provides nourishment and solace to friends and relatives in need. You're good, sturdy, reliable people when times are hard, and interesting, entertaining company in times of plenty.

What more could any marriage hope for?

The Cancer Marriage

(JUNE 22–JULY 23)

Famous Sun-in-Cancer Marriages

Richard and Pat Nixon (June 21)
Ben Affleck and Jennifer Garner (June 29)
Ozzy and Sharon Osbourne (July 4)
Rosalynn and Jimmy Carter (July 7)

❧❀❧

A friend of mine tells the story of a relative—we'll call him Uncle Jeffrey—who brought his new bride home to meet his family. When the new bride met with a chilly reception from his siblings, Uncle Jeffrey muttered a terse "Right"—and spirited his bride away to another hemisphere. He never returned to the country of his birth.

I like to think Uncle Jeffrey was married when the Sun was in Cancer. When he got married, he didn't just take a wife: he chose her to be his family.

Every new marriage creates a new family unit. If you doubt it, you haven't been married very long. Now, forming a new family unit is bound to cause a little tension between the two of you and the families in which you were raised. You will create new traditions and rituals that may supersede those you grew up with. You may decide to live in a different city or to pursue a very different lifestyle. Eventually, you may decide to raise children and do it quite differently from the way both of you were raised.

The idea of creating a family unit is fundamental to the Cancer marriage. You are the couple that takes care of the aging relatives because they have taken care of you; that provides a nurturing halfway house for confused teens; that cooks traditional family recipes and treasures the family heirlooms and history, perhaps tracking the genealogy of both families. You respect your families and want them to be part of your lives.

All of these kindnesses notwithstanding, there is a steely protectiveness at the core of your marriage. No one will get very far by interfering in your own family's affairs; in fact, anyone who tries will find themselves on the receiving end of the Uncle Jeffrey treatment.

The Cancer Season

The Sun moves through Cancer between late June and late July. The Sun's entry into Cancer marks the summer solstice, the longest day of the year and the official beginning of summer. In the United States, Independence Day is celebrated on July 4 and provides a federal holiday around which to organize vacation time. And so we've come to associate summer with family: holidays at the seashore, with kids playing in the waves while Mom and Dad relax on the sand; hours spent driving across country to visit relatives or far-flung attractions such as theme parks; barbecues and parades. It's also a time when children go away to camp and experience their first bouts of homesickness.

The marriage that begins during the Cancer season carries the seeds of that summer warmth, and nurtures them in a protective cocoon of family togetherness. Often, one partner plays an almost parental role with the other—for instance, Sharon Osbourne has been a legendarily fierce protector of her husband, rock star Ozzy Osbourne. The Osbourne's short-lived "reality" series on MTV reflected the Cancerian spirit of their marriage in its title sequence with its nostalgic "Father Knows Best" theme.

Cancer marriages tend to follow rather conventional gender roles, but this is not to imply that the women are shrinking violets or the men swaggering Neanderthals. "The woman behind the man"—Sharon Osbourne, Rosalynn Carter, Pat Nixon—is a formidable presence in the Cancer marriage, often playing a strong supporting role to a gentle (Jimmy Carter), flawed (Richard Nixon), or even slightly befuddled (Ozzy) husband.

How It Begins: The Cancer Wedding

Cancer likes its parties cozy, intimate, traditional, and close to home. Cancer is the sign that rules family, so if you wed during this season, wear your grandmother's dress or a piece of heirloom jewelry. Hold your ceremony or reception at someone's home—but avoid, perhaps, using the home of either of your mothers. When Venus in Cancer—the sign of motherhood—flies off the rails, it can play the role of the possessive, meddling mother-in-law better than anyone.

Cancer is the sign that rules nourishment, so guests will pay a lot of attention to the food that is served. And it is a sensitive sign, so pre-wedding emotions will run high, with tearful quarrels and an overwrought bride teetering on the brink of bridezilladom. Even more than most weddings, this one is all about the ladies; gentlemen should just step back and try not to get in the way. But don't step back too far. Normally the most nurturing and considerate of signs, Cancer can turn sulky in a hurry when it doesn't feel appreciated!

Cancer is associated with the colors of the Moon, its ruling "planet"—iridescent silvers, grays and blue-grays, white, and palest yellow. For flowers, choose blooms that symbolize tradition and romance. Cancer is especially partial to flowers with an antique/Victorian feel such as the rose, iris, and Queen Anne's lace. Basically, if it would look at home in the lobby of a Victorian bed-and-breakfast inn, it will suit your Cancer wedding.

The Care and Feeding of Your Cancer Marriage

THE PURPOSE OF A CANCER MARRIAGE

The marriage that begins when the Sun is in Cancer is primarily a marriage of **nurturing**. As a team, you are always at your best when you are providing sustenance—food, comfort, and emotional support. No one says, "Aw, poor baby" in quite so comforting a way as Cancer. You enjoy creating an environment that nurtures, comforts, and takes care of people.

Your home will likely be dominated by a huge dining table, where on any given night of the week, friends, neighbors, and assorted family members can be found sharing a meal. When your loved ones need a shoulder to cry on, yours are the shoulders they seek. Like surrogate parents, you'll help them move, cook them casseroles, and tell them what to do—whether or not they want your advice!

WHAT THE CANCER MARRIAGE NEEDS

You need to feel **safe**. You need to feel that you're part of a family. You need to take care of people. And although you will never, ever admit this, you need to feel appreciated for all the things you do for others. It's not exactly that you feel people *owe* you anything for your kindness and attention; it's that you are extremely sensitive to the notion that unscrupulous sorts might take advantage of you. Quite apart from the very human wish to not look like chumps, you are keenly aware that you only have so much energy, time, and money to go around—and you want it to be used for the benefit of those people for whom you care most deeply.

SOURCES OF FRICTION

When you don't feel appreciated, you withdraw. At worst, you reinforce each other's feelings of woundedness and seek to punish those who haven't given you the love and gratitude you feel you deserve. If you're not careful about nurturing each other, this resentfulness can extend to your partner.

You can also be a little overprotective of one another, which is okay for some personalities—say, a Cancer, a Taurus, or even a Scorpio—but decidedly not for those with a strong independent streak. A Cancer marriage is a tough row to hoe for your garden-variety Aries, Gemini, Sagittarius, Capricorn, or Aquarius. If you are freedom-loving types, it may be helpful to think about ways in which you can *nurture autonomy* in your relationship. A good mother gives her children both roots and wings. A good Cancer marriage does the same—offers both partners a place to feel safe and a sturdy platform from which to launch out into the world on dazzling adventures.

The Cancer Marriage Style

THE FACE YOU SHOW THE WORLD

As a couple, you're a little shy about the limelight. Big, glitzy parties aren't generally your thing. You are happiest meeting the world on your own turf, preferably your home; and when you connect with new people, you do so by making them feel at home and like "one of the family." You're the *de facto* parental figures among your group of friends and associates—even if you are fairly unconventional parents, like the Osbournes!

WHAT YOU OWN

You are quite generous with your money, and are happy to share it with those you love. You consider money to be worth very little if it doesn't provide fun and happiness, so you are also willing to open the purse strings for concert and theater tickets. You are inclined to pay extra for good-quality furnishings for your home, and like your possessions to reflect your good taste and social standing.

You have a weakness for toys, and will likely fill your home with gadgets and games—a pool table, an antique jukebox, a big-screen television. Personal grooming—massage, skin treatments, even plastic surgery—are other services that you consider worthwhile investments.

HOW YOU COMMUNICATE

Cancer has a reputation as a bit of a scold—a nag, if you will. And it's true that you are apt to be a bit critical in the way you communicate, both with one another and with the rest of the world. You're extremely smart, capable people, very detail-oriented, with a great deal of practical ability in problem-solving. But your standards are high, and it's all too easy for you to fall into the habit of pointing out where others fall short and offering unsolicited advice.

If you can avoid the tendency to criticize and meddle, your ability to combine practical assistance with emotional support is an irresistible combination. What could be more lovable than a couple who will fix your computer while feeding you a cookie and letting you sob on their shoulders about your lost data?

HOW YOU LIVE

People are often surprised when they see the inside of your home for the first time. Because there is a whiff of the old-fashioned and romantic about you, they expect to find a home filled with chintz and lace curtains. Instead, they are likely to find classic, even modern furnishings. Gentle colors, inviting fabrics, sophisticated artwork and music, and soft lighting create an atmosphere of peaceful refinement where voices are not raised, interactions are liberally peppered with "please" and "thank you," and arguments are discouraged.

Yours is a home designed for entertaining and for greeting the world. When you choose, decorate, or remodel a home, the primary consideration is that the space be able to accommodate large groups of people in a gracious manner. Southern antebellum hospitality—in which enormous plantation houses were maintained to accommodate any number of guests for as long as months at a time—is your ideal, but you'll settle for one fully dedicated guest bedroom with a powder room full of thirsty towels and scented soaps.

YOUR CHILDREN AND CREATIVE SPIRIT

Though your house is graceful and serene, your children tend to be anything but quiet and polite! These are shrewd, observant young people who delight in asking difficult and embarrassing questions, who are fascinated by taboo subjects from an early age, and who throw fits and swear like sailors. Their taste in music, bedroom décor, and friends runs toward the most shocking and unsettling.

Your task as parents to such children is surprisingly simple: be truthful, be consistent, and be firm. It is because you have created a secure environment for your children from birth that they feel secure enough to dabble into life's dark and difficult side. But if they go too far, don't hesitate to go straight into meddling parent mode and pull them back toward the light.

If you don't have children, you will doubtless have extreme and unusual pets and/or hobbies that you pursue with near-fanatical zeal. You have enormous creative energy and the ability to produce art, writing, music, or any other craft with depth and exceptional beauty. You are quiet and self-protective in many areas of your marriage, but in your art you are fearless.

YOUR WORK, HEALTH, AND DAILY ROUTINE
You're not slaves to routine, preferring to take each day as it comes. You generally prefer work that stretches the mind, such as teaching or research, but especially like such work when it takes you outdoors (or on the road) on a regular basis.

You may also work in a support capacity for those in education, science, law, or publishing. Editing, running tests using machines, or developing testing methods are likely areas of work for you both.

You may have a cavalier attitude toward your health, but can improve your chances of remaining healthy by getting plenty of outdoor exercise, whether hiking, walking, or gardening.

YOUR FRIENDS AND FOES

Because you present a façade of tenderness and nurturing, your friends tend to be tough, worldly characters who are fiercely protective of you. Successful, high-powered career types are especially likely to find their way to your home for a hearty meal and a diverting evening with you and your intriguing children.

But beware: Your predilection for giving can occasionally make you the targets of those with a penchant for taking. When your relationships with others begin to seem one-sided, practice asking for something in return. Prompting a frequent dinner guest to bring along a loaf of special bread or bottle of wine is a symbolic gesture that reminds both parties that relationships work best when both sides bring something to the table.

WHAT YOU SHARE

You're shrewd at managing your investments, resistant to carrying debt, and a little bit kinky in the bedroom. For all your closeness and your protectiveness, you are actually quite adept at providing each other with a certain sense of independence—and that keeps your relationship interesting and compelling.

You truly loathe and distrust being in anyone's debt. You don't like credit cards, and you pay your mortgage off as early as humanly possible. When you rely on others to provide for you, it makes you feel insecure, and that's intolerable to you.

WHAT YOU BELIEVE

You're not necessarily conventionally religious, but you do consider yourselves deeply spiritual. You are tenderhearted toward those in need, and your heart goes out to nations around the world that cannot feed or defend their people. In all likelihood, your studies in school included a healthy dose of multiculturalism, particularly if you went to college.

Your feelings about multiculturalism are conflicted. On one hand, nothing is as appealing to you as your own culture, home, and hearth. But on the other hand, you probably adore ethnic food, art, music, and fashion. In the end, you may feel most comfortable encountering different cultures on your own turf—or by traveling abroad with a familiar entourage.

YOUR CONTRIBUTION TO THE WORLD

You are particularly apt to be entrepreneurs or small business owners. Because your drive for security is very strong, you aren't content to sit around and wait for someone else to offer you business opportunities—you prefer to create them yourselves. A home-based business is a very likely scenario for you, one in which you provide the kind of technical support, publicity, or editing services described in the "work, health, and daily routine" section.

You are very assertive, driven business people, but because your family unit is your foremost priority, you will seek to create business opportunities that keep you close to home—and, eventually, bring your children into the business if they so choose. In contrast to the warm, maternal quality of your personal life, in business you can drive others pretty hard—though not as hard as you drive yourselves.

YOUR PLACE IN SOCIETY

You are truly giving, caring people, and your social circle and connections with the community reflect these traits. Your most intimate friends tend to be worldly, ambitious types, often work associates or old family friends; but for socializing you enjoy people with simple tastes and pleasures, who enjoy nothing better than a lively evening by your fire. You meet these associates through your appreciation of the arts, food, or perhaps gardening.

You're not, generally speaking, visionaries; you have no grand design for your lives. You prefer to enjoy the present, bask in the love of your family and friends, and trust that the future will take care of itself.

YOUR PRIVATE SANCTUARY

Secretly, when no one else is looking, you're gossips. When people tell you their problems in confidence, you respect that confidence—except with each other. You take in a lot of juicy gossip in the course of a day, and it's all fodder for some juicy pillow talk when you go to bed at night.

You're also a lot more intellectually curious than most people guess. When you're home alone, you're often dipping into huge piles of books and magazines, perhaps journaling, studying languages, or learning some new skill. People who know only your practical and caretaking sides are startled when you announce one day that one of you has written a novel, or when you suddenly begin conversing with each other in fluent French. Just because you're homebodies doesn't mean your minds don't do a lot of traveling!

The Leo Marriage

(JULY 24–AUGUST 23)

Famous Sun-in-Leo Marriages

Prince Charles and Princess Diana (July 29)
Anne Bancroft and Mel Brooks (August 5)
Sting and Trudie Styler (August 20)
Frida Kahlo and Diego Rivera (August 21)

❧❦❧

*M*y parents were farmers who were born, raised, and married in rural Indiana. In short, they were not Sting and Trudie Styler, or Frida Kahlo and Diego Rivera, or even Anne Bancroft and Mel Brooks. They didn't sing or play instruments, paint pictures, or produce and act in films. But when you look at Polaroids taken of my parents in the 1950s and 1960s, when they were in their twenties and thirties, you can't take your eyes off of them. Whether it was my exuberant mother in her bright red lipstick and pedal pushers, Dad with his shirt sleeves rolled up to show off muscled forearms, or the two of them dressed to kill for a night at the local fraternal lodge, they were drop-dead gorgeous people. People with raw, animal magnetism and a palpable zest for life.

By the time my sister and I came along, my parents—who married when my mother was only sixteen years old—had had nearly a decade to work the kinks out of their marriage; we never saw them argue. My brothers, however, remember quite a different marriage full of passionate arguments born of a profound difference in their natures, for my father was as taciturn as my mother was outgoing. For all of us, though, Mom and Dad were the dazzling nucleus of our little solar system—gorgeous, magnetic, and passionate.

Needless to say, they were married in mid-August, when the Sun was in Leo. I often refer to the Leo marriage as a "rock star" marriage, a characterization that troubles Pamela, my modest Pisces friend who married in late July. I certainly don't mean to imply that Leo marriages are full of scissor-kicking Mick Jagger clones in spandex trousers who live flamboyant lives full of groupies and debauchery. Rather, I mean there is a glamour to the Leo marriage couple, an irresistible gravitational pull that draws others to them.

If you married with the Sun in Leo, you're a couple with a gift for fun, with an aura of being truly present and involved in every gathering, every activity, every relationship. No party really begins until you show up. It's a powerful gift, this kind of "couple charisma," and it carries with it an obligation: to inspire everyone you meet to love passionately and to live their own lives with creative vigor and enthusiasm.

The Leo Season

The Sun is in Leo between late July and the third week in August—the height of summer in the Northern Hemisphere and the middle of winter down under. The extremes in temperature make it an unpopular time of year to marry in climates that are already hot and humid; no one wants to be a wilting bride. On the other hand, for older couples established in certain professions (academia, mental health fields) this may be the only time of year they can easily get away for a wedding ceremony and honeymoon.

Leo, a passionate and creative fire sign, is legendarily given to grand romantic gestures. Leo *loves to be in love* and, while inherently loyal, is susceptible to flattery. Henry VIII, though a Cancer, was surely born with a heavy Leo signature to his chart, with his womanizing and dramatic wooing, writing songs for his lovers, and impressing them with dances and feasts.

The Leo marriage is especially suitable for artists, musicians, and other creative folks. The Leo household is especially popular with young people; if you have children, their friends will be drawn to your house. If you don't have children, younger relatives will be magnetized by the aura of warmth and fun that surrounds your home.

How It Begins: The Leo Wedding

Leo, the ruling sign of pageantry, divas, and royalty, heralds a wedding that is less solemn ritual than lavish, off-Broadway production. Every aspect of the wedding and reception will be carefully (even excessively) thought out and will be calibrated to the highest possible level of creativity and dramatic effect.

Leo is cheerful, magnanimous, and above all, dignified. Every luxury and treat will be provided to make guests feel pampered and impressed by the couple's good taste. There will be at least one guest who plays the role of "life of the party," leading the conga line and setting a playful tone that is downright infectious. (Think of the irrepressible Gareth in *Four Weddings and a Funeral*.) But woe to the guest who steps out of line and embarrasses the wedding couple with tasteless jokes or drunken excess. The dignified wedding couple will let him know, in the words of Queen Victoria, that "We are not amused."

Color your Leo wedding in all the shades of fire: golds, yellows, oranges, reds, tawny browns. Leo favors classic styling (think Italian), but is more than happy to embrace color and patterns, the bolder the better. Drape your reception tables in contrasting shades of fiery silk; let your bridesmaids choose gowns that represent all the colors of the sun—gold, yellow, orange, red.

For flowers, exotic, dramatic, and unusual blooms are the favored choice for a Leo wedding. Gardenia, freesia, gladiola, iris, larkspur, lily of the valley, roses, snapdragons, and sunflowers—anything that is fragrant and distinctive is a suitable complement to a regal couple on their dazzling day.

The Care and Feeding of Your Leo Marriage

THE PURPOSE OF A LEO MARRIAGE

The Leo marriage has an evolutionary imperative to **inspire**—each other, your families and friends, and your community. You are natural leaders, because your confidence in your individual visions is infectious. You always seem to be having a good time and doing interesting things, and you carry them out with such flair and élan that others can't help but be intrigued and inspired by your example.

Leo also has a managerial side, and likes to organize group activities—lavish dinner parties, plays and concerts, fundraising events, games, and contests. Leo's job is to make life fun and exciting, and you instinctively understand that any party is a lot more enjoyable when the host has carefully organized enough food, drink, and comfortable seating for everyone.

WHAT THE LEO MARRIAGE NEEDS

Simply, **self-expression**. Leo has a reputation for being self-centered and greedy for attention, but while a couple in a Leo marriage likes to be noticed, what you really *need* is to be engaged in passionate pursuits. Your partner can never be the source of all your passion; each of you needs to be passionately devoted not only to each other, but to your individual interests, especially creative endeavors. Neglect this part of your marriage at your peril. The more interested you both are in life itself, the more interesting you remain to one another.

SOURCES OF FRICTION

The same passion and sex appeal that make your marriage so exciting also make each of you enticing to other people. Your marriage is uniquely vulnerable to interference from interested third parties, but your fidelity to one another is vulnerable only when you forget to nurture the romance, drama, and passion in your own marriage. Flirtations with other people are natural within any relationship, but can easily become a problem if either of you is insecure or suspicious.

Your marriage will generally attract a lot of attention and social opportunities, and while this can be flattering, a very full social schedule can actually be quite overwhelming to people who are naturally introverted. Keep in mind that just as royalty and celebrities keep body-guards and secretaries around to protect their privacy, it's perfectly all right for the two of you to turn down the occasional invitation and enjoy a quiet evening at home.

The Leo Marriage Style

THE FACE YOU SHOW THE WORLD

The Leo marriage is built on creativity and a sense of social performance. You're warm and fun and have great presence; parties come alive when you walk in, and everything takes on a heightened luster. You tend to be the "it" couple of your social circle, the one that everyone wants at their dinner parties, and if you can't make it to social engagements, they often don't happen at all.

WHAT YOU OWN

You present such a generous face to the world that your fiscal restraint tends to take people by surprise. You believe in using resources wisely and frugally, recycling, limiting your driving, clipping coupons, and eating a diet low in red meat and high in grains.

If anything, you worry too much about money and can become somewhat preoccupied by the subject. You certainly have the skills and resourcefulness necessary to earn a good living, and it's to your credit that you are careful about spending and saving. But beware of talking too much about your fiscal affairs, especially criticizing others for taking a different approach.

HOW YOU COMMUNICATE

You're perfectly lovely conversationalists, and your ability to draw others out with graceful questions and witty anecdotes is a large part of your popularity as a couple. It's not that you never argue—in fact, you rather enjoy presenting opposing points of view to each other and to the world—but that you tend to argue in the classical sense, exchanging views, not verbal blows.

Your siblings probably play an important role in your relationship. Often one of them introduced you to one another or in some other way helped bring you together. But it's communication that keeps you together; you really enjoy talking to each other, and may also communicate through music, art, or poetry.

HOW YOU LIVE

Magic: that's the word for your home. Filled with dramatic colors, patterns, art, and music, your home has sex appeal. Given your warm social presence, it's perhaps a little surprising that you don't host more parties at home, but you welcome family and close friends for intimate gatherings. You guard your privacy, and are unlikely to become very close to your neighbors. If at all possible, you avoid boarders and even long-term guests.

Your domestic style is exotic, with patchouli incense scenting the air and lots of sumptuous, inviting fabrics. You're not necessarily apt to do much cooking at home, but when you do, the meals will be spicy, hot, and full of strong flavors.

YOUR CHILDREN AND CREATIVE SPIRIT

You are one of the couples who is a bit more likely than usual to devote your creative energies to art, travel, or academia rather than raising children. This may not be your choice, necessarily; the world is full of couples who would dearly love children of their own but are unable to reproduce or to adopt.

You are resilient and upbeat by nature, though, and you will certainly use your creative powers in many ways. You are also likely to be involved with young people through teaching or mentorship.

YOUR WORK, HEALTH, AND DAILY ROUTINE

You tend to be conscientious in both work and health habits, and are therefore apt to rise to positions of authority and leadership, and to live into healthy old age. Your danger zone is overwork, and neglecting the need for recreation to balance your hard work. When you do leave work behind and throw yourselves enthusiastically into recreational activities, you may be especially vulnerable to sprains, breaks, and back problems after long periods of physical inactivity at a desk. Be sure to stretch well before playing!

Mundane daily tasks are not terribly interesting to you; you'd rather work a bit harder so you can afford to hire others to assume some of life's least congenial tasks, like cleaning the house or mowing the lawn.

YOUR FRIENDS AND FOES

Those you consider your true intimates are wildly independent, iconoclastic rebels and eccentrics. You like a lot of space in your personal relationships, including within your marriage. It's important for you to feel as though people are with you because they adore you, and not because they need something from you. People who are radical, inventive thinkers and who have passionate interests and lots of friends are exactly the right companions for you.

The people who are most likely to wish you harm are similarly off-beat, but they lack the centering core of sanity and humanity that you and your true friends have in common. It's a fine line between eccentric and crazy, and you will experience your share of both. More than any other couple, you are apt to attract lunatics into your midst; they practically show up on your doorstep out of thin air, begging to be let in.

WHAT YOU SHARE

You are true romantics, and your intimate lives have the quality of a romance novel. You tend to blend together in a very natural way until people really do relate to you much more as a couple than as individuals. Part of the fairy-tale, rock-star mythology of your marriage has to do precisely with this quality of romance and inseparability.

When it comes to the practical aspects of sharing your lives together, you are similarly enmeshed. You're not, for instance, the kind of couple that is likely to maintain separate bank accounts or vacation without each other.

WHAT YOU BELIEVE

You adore travel to foreign lands, and the more foreign they are, the better. You will probably live abroad at some point during your marriage, and be considered pioneers by those close to you for your energetic pursuit of new experiences. You strongly believe that the world is meant to be explored.

You are the consummate charmers in social situations, but you are forces to be reckoned with on the subjects of religion and politics. You are passionate, opinionated, even reckless on these subjects, and are quite possibly activists for one or a number of causes. You are warriors of the mind.

YOUR CONTRIBUTION TO THE WORLD

People instinctively trust you; you seem solid and respectable, un-shockable and dependable. You do well in careers that require you to calm people down, rather like a lion tamer in a circus. You tend to fall into career grooves of astonishing longevity, working in one place for decades, or working away diligently at a particular skill or goal and reaching it after many years of persistence. It doesn't matter particularly what your career or business (for you are highly likely to be in business for yourself) is, although you may be likely to be involved in cultivating resources—art, agriculture, banking, beauty services. What is more impressive than the kind of work you do is the way you do it: slowly, steadily, methodically, which is so unexpected for so magnetic and flashy a couple.

YOUR PLACE IN SOCIETY

Your natural allies are mischief makers and wits, and they all share one thing in common: they are absolutely delightful conversationalists. You want friends who are entertaining and smart, who do a lot of things well, and who have lots and lots of other friends—you don't like other people to rely on you too much, although you are infinitely trustworthy.

You don't tend to be long-range thinkers. You prefer a series of short-term goals that may eventually add up to something of more consequence. Almost certainly your vision consists of many different interests and activities, like a house with many rooms, all of them decorated in a different style.

YOUR PRIVATE SANCTUARY

Because you appear incredibly confident, magnetic, and radiant, few people guess that you have a sensitive, home-loving side. You are deeply hurt by social slights, and although your generosity to others is given spontaneously and freely, you are injured when others don't show gratitude or offer the same treatment in return.

You're not the type of couple to wear your emotions on your sleeves. You can be worried, sick, suffering, or upset, and few people outside your marriage will know. Part of the reason is the legendary Leo pride:

you never want to appear weak or needy. But you are also extremely sensitive, and the less people know about your private affairs, the safer you feel. You prefer to retire to your lair to gather strength, then return to the world stronger than ever.

The Virgo Marriage

Famous Sun-in-Virgo Marriages

John F. Kennedy and Jacqueline Kennedy (Sept. 12)
Robert and Elizabeth Barrett Browning (Sept. 12)
Gene Wilder and Gilda Radner (Sept. 18)
John Kennedy Jr. and Carolyn Bessette (Sept. 21)

❧

I've spent years working with wedding couples to choose their wedding dates using astrology. The first thing I tell them before we begin the process is this: there are no perfect wedding dates, and there are no perfect marriages, because there are no perfect people. Choosing a wedding date with astrology is a terrific litmus test of a couple's readiness to marry, because it requires compromise. The nearly perfect wedding date doesn't work logistically, or the logistics of their situation require that they marry at an absolutely awful moment astrologically. One or the other has to give; some couples accept this easily and philosophically. Others, to put it gently, do not.

And I understand this because the dream of a perfect marriage dies hard. Look at the examples of famous marriages included at the top of this page—they read like a list of fairy tales. JFK and Jackie and JFK Jr. and Carolyn Bessette could not have been more photo-friendly—impossibly gorgeous, timelessly elegant figures who looked like they belonged on top of a wedding cake. The marriage of Gene Wilder and Gilda Radner is essentially the story of a heroic, supportive husband who nursed his ailing wife and went on to do good works in her name. But it's worth noting that not only did each of these marriages end tragically, but their fairy-tale mythologies were an illusion. JFK indulged in serial adultery and was assassinated. His son and daughter-in-law by some accounts fought bitterly and perished together in the waters of the Atlantic. Gilda Radner lost her battle with cancer, and Gene Wilder's subsequent memoir included surprisingly bitter recollections of their marriage.

My point, I hasten to assure you, is NOT that the Virgo marriage is doomed to adultery, arguing, or premature death! Rather, it's that no matter how perfect it may appear on the outside, no marriage is perfect on the inside. And living with this, and loving each other despite all imperfections of character and of your union, is the key to a happy and satisfying Virgo marriage.

The Virgo Season

The Sun is in Virgo between late August and late September—technically late summer, but forever autumn in the memories of those of us who returned to school just after Labor Day each year. The Virgo season marks the moment of evaluating crops to calculate the precise moment when their harvest will produce the greatest yield. Is there a perfect time to bring in the crops? No. Just a judiciously rendered opinion. Virgo, then, symbolizes appraisal and educated guesswork.

In myth, Virgo seems most akin to Demeter, goddess of the harvest. Demeter was independent and self-contained with all the bounty of the earth at her disposal, and seems to have been the only god or goddess who was deeply involved with the day-to-day affairs of humankind.

In the mythical Demeter we see Virgo's association with the harvest and also with work, analysis, and daily routine. The astrological Virgo symbolizes hands-on craftsmanship as well as the wise analysis of resources and their best use. When a marriage begins with the Sun in Virgo, we expect a union that produces good work, emphasizes the wise use of resources, and yet is generous in response to need.

How It Begins: The Virgo Wedding

Simple, classic, elegant: your Virgo wedding ceremony begins with the essentials necessary to make your ceremony legal and binding— the two of you, a license, and an officiant—and builds carefully, cautiously, and prudently. Virgo is a health-conscious, environmentally friendly, animal-loving sign. It's not unusual for the Virgo wedding to take place outdoors, for the invitations to be printed on recycled paper with soy ink, and for the reception buffet to offer vegan options.

Ideal venues include parks, beaches, vineyards, or even a zoo. Music tends toward the simple and unadorned—an acoustic guitar, a flute, a single voice. Like Gemini, its Mercury-ruled kin, Virgo loves language, so your ceremony will almost certainly feature eloquent readings and vows composed by the two of you.

Virgo is associated with earthy, conservative colors—dark shades of blue, navy in particular; butternut; and neutrals such as tan and cream. Virgo also has an affinity for texture and discreet use of pattern, such as damask or pinstripe fabric, or a cake iced with a basketweave pattern.

Like fellow earth signs Taurus and Capricorn, Virgo adores flowers and plants of all kinds, and favors loose, natural arrangements of the simplest blooms. Flowers commonly associated with Virgo are aster, chrysanthemum, and morning glory, but for table centerpieces and altar decoration, consider live potted plants, which can be taken home by guests as keepsakes and replanted in their gardens.

The Care and Feeding of Your Virgo Marriage

THE PURPOSE OF A VIRGO MARRIAGE

The marriage that begins when the Sun is in Virgo is primarily a marriage of **service**. As a team, you are always at your best when you are providing practical assistance to the people around you, helping them untangle life's knottiest problems. Your families and friends turn to you when a computer's hard drive fails, a car starts making mysterious noises, or a bookcase needs to be assembled. Virgo has an instinctive feel for such tasks, as well as for more abstract duties such as balancing the books, cutting through red tape, and teaching a kid geometry.

If someone—or some animal—you love is sick or suffering, you will immediately be on the scene to provide practical aid and cool comfort. You are the backbone of your favorite charity, your kids' school, and your community center. You're not afraid to pick up trash, stuff envelopes, or do anything else that will make your highest ideals of purity, order, and efficiency achievable in the real world.

WHAT THE VIRGO MARRIAGE NEEDS

You need to feel needed, and you need to feel you are making a practical contribution to the people and causes you care about. You suffer more than most couples when your jobs are unsatisfying or seem meaningless. At the end of the day, you need to see tangible results for your efforts—a clean house, a bound report, a bandaged patient.

SOURCES OF FRICTION

Because you have a knack for figuring out how things work, you also have a talent for figuring out *what's wrong*—with a process, a situation, or a person. What would make it function better, more efficiently? You always have an opinion. But remember: your advice is most helpful when it has been requested; your help is most valuable when it addresses what other people need or want as opposed to what you think they need or want; and when it comes to people, helping them function more efficiently should not be your end game. Rather, focus on learning how to more perfectly cherish the people you love.

The Virgo Marriage Style

THE FACE YOU SHOW THE WORLD

The Virgo marriage meets life with a sense of practical purpose, modesty, and the impulse to figure out how to make a situation *work*. Your marriage encourages the two of you to constantly explore ways to be helpful; you're quick to charge to the rescue when a friend's car is on the blink, and you're among the first to volunteer to help a young relative move into his first apartment. You're not flashy, and don't expect to be lauded for your helpful impulses and actions. Rather, you gain real satisfaction from restoring a machine to working order or unloading dozens of cardboard cartons into a third-floor walk-up. However … resist the urge to offer unsolicited advice, or to criticize, even in the name of being truthful.

WHAT YOU OWN

Management of resources is an area of life in which your partnership shines. Virgo is practical and wants to use money, property, energy, and all other resources in a way that does the least harm to the planet while providing optimal benefit. You are a financial team, even if one of you takes the lead in earning or managing money for both of you. You are likely to earn a good living in careers that emphasize counseling, public relations, or arbitration, because you encourage a keen sense of fairness and diplomacy in one another.

It would be unusual for yours to be a single-income marriage, because it's vital for you both to feel as though you're contributing equally to your marriage's bottom line. It's likely that at least one of you earns a living in the arts, fashion, sales, finance or property appraisal, or public relations. You rarely spend much on luxury items, but you happily open the purse strings for music, art, beautiful objects for your home, and gifts for each other.

HOW YOU COMMUNICATE

Fearless is the best possible description of the communication between you. If you are able to talk about absolutely anything with each other, without fear of manipulation or criticism, you will consider your marriage a big success. If, on the other hand, you keep secrets from one another, you will be expressing the worst possible reaction to the communicative energy of your marriage.

The criticisms you withhold in your other relationships flow freely within your marriage. Unless one of you is very prideful or sensitive, this mode of expression—while it may seem a little rough from the outside—suits you quite well. Better, certainly, that you are brutally honest with one another, since it's unlikely that you'll be able to keep secrets from one another.

HOW YOU LIVE

You like a spacious home that requires as little maintenance as possible. You will happily sacrifice square footage, though, for an expansive view of sky and trees and enough acreage to keep a menagerie of animals. Pets—and nature—are what make a home for you. If your outdoor spaces are nonexistent or unsatisfactory, you will be restless and ill-at-ease, constantly itching to move on. You're most at home in a meadow adjoining a forest, with majestic mountains in the distance and a river running through it all, but you'll settle for a big house on a generous plot of land.

It's likely that you will make your home some distance from your families, or at least limit the time you spend with them. Together, you enjoy exploring activities, foods, and pastimes that are quite different from those you grew up with. For all your frugality and practical approach to life, your home tends to be a loud, merry, informal place with plenty of lively color and clutter.

YOUR CHILDREN AND CREATIVE SPIRIT

You may make your careers in fields related to children or the arts. Or you may choose to have no children at all. If you do have them, you will take the responsibility seriously. They will be well educated, beautifully behaved, and responsible from an early age—little adults in children's bodies!

Your hobbies and recreational interests lean toward the creation of practical, useful things. You might enjoy gardening, building models, sculpting, weaving, home repair, or other handicrafts. You tend to enjoy the planning phase of a task and the satisfaction of its results more than the actual work itself, and your idea of an enjoyable day of leisure is to draft up a list of tasks and spend your day crossing them off.

YOUR WORK, HEALTH, AND DAILY ROUTINE

You have some offbeat, even radical ideas about work, and are happiest as entrepreneurs, as business owners, or in jobs that take you into the field on a regular basis. Sitting at the same desk in the same office day after day is not what you were made to do. If you find work that allows you freedom and variety, you will be happy to stay with it for the long haul. Best of all, a regular routine—even a rather strange one—will keep you healthy.

Despite the generally robust health that your marriage encourages, you may find you are prone to allergies, touchy digestion, and skin irritations. Most likely this is a consequence of nervous energy and mental processes that are difficult to switch off; you simply don't relax very effectively. Spending time with friends who make you laugh can help, and taking baths, or keeping some water feature such as a birdbath, fish tank, or fountain around your house, may be soothing and grounding for you both.

YOUR FRIENDS AND FOES

Because you are pragmatic, sensible, and linear in your approach to life, your friends tend to be people who balance that approach with a more inspired, easy-going, flexible perspective. They help you "get out of your heads" and live in the moment, and you in turn lend practical assistance and analytical insight when necessary.

On occasion, though, your combined energy will tend to attract those whose lives are completely chaotic, unorganized, and careening out of control. These are people who are desperately in need of practical assistance and a strong support system, and you are uniquely qualified to offer this kind of help. On the other hand, some people's lives are out of control because of choices they've made and an unwillingness to face reality. In situations like these, your efforts to help might exacerbate rather than relieve the problem. Beware of becoming addicted to rescuing others; it's not healthy for anyone involved.

WHAT YOU SHARE

Your relationship is much more passionate than most people suspect—after all, Virgo is an earth sign and delights in the pleasures of physical intimacy. But yours tends to be the kind of passion that is accompanied by arguments and even competition with one another.

Though you're generally pretty conservative in your spending, you're aggressive investors, if a bit impulsive. You do best at managing shared resources such as bank accounts and investments when one of you is placed firmly in charge of these things; it's not an area of your relationship that lends itself easily to cooperation between you.

WHAT YOU BELIEVE

All things being equal, this isn't a marriage that encourages religious zeal, academic ambition, or extensive world travel. If these things were of deep interest in your lives before marriage, they will likely stay that way—but your marriage alone is unlikely to increase your interest. Yours is a practical view of the universe, and your religious view can come down to the simple theory "enjoy everything."

You will study and earn advanced degrees if you need to for practical reasons, and will likely travel for pleasure but probably not often. You're generally a bit wary of the unfamiliar and prefer to limit yourselves to a few favorite restaurants, cultural activities, and vacation spots.

YOUR CONTRIBUTION TO THE WORLD

You both, almost certainly, have careers, and perhaps more than one apiece, or a few hobbies that are as compelling and time consuming as your occupations. You would do well in communication-related fields such as marketing, writing, advertising, or sales, but really your skill with words and ideas will serve you well in any field.

Your siblings are likely to influence your career choices or to be involved in your work, whether inspiring you to pursue a particular direction, helping you find job opportunities or clients, or working alongside you in your profession.

YOUR PLACE IN SOCIETY

You can be impatient and prickly if you are feeling stressed out, over-worked, and underappreciated, but you have a seriously clucky side that comes out with your friends. You like to feed them, take care of them, and give them advice about their problems. Mostly, this is benign and even appreciated. But when taken to excess, or in combination with your tendency toward criticism, the effect can be a bit stifling.

You're capable of long-term planning, mainly in relation to security and plans for your children or your retirement, and are likely to make real estate investments the cornerstone of your retirement plan. Above all, you want to make sure you will be able to remain in your own home well into old age.

You're a socially conscious duo and are often involved with social organizations, particularly those devoted to relieving world hunger or providing shelter (such as Habitat for Humanity) and relating to women's issues, including reproductive health.

YOUR PRIVATE SANCTUARY

On the surface, you're modest and self-deprecating. But scratch the surface and it's as though you were Caesar and Cleopatra in a past life and never quite got over it. In the privacy of your own home, your relationship is drama central, with plenty of arguments, laughter, and role playing. Music, games, movies, and crafts are your favorite escapes for rest and renewal. You may also have artistic talents that you prefer to keep private for fear that expressing them may cause others to take you less seriously. When you need to relax and restore your energy, indulging these creative talents can be exactly what you need.

The Libra Marriage

Famous Sun-in-Libra Marriages

Bill and Hillary Clinton (Oct 11)
Kate Capshaw and Steven Spielberg (October 12)
Gerald R. and Betty Ford (October 15)
Barack and Michelle Obama (October 18)

❧

*W*as there ever an onscreen marriage more realistic and utterly captivating than that of Adam and Amanda Bonner, as portrayed by Spencer Tracey and Katharine Hepburn in 1949's *Adam's Rib*? The Bonners, both attorneys, have the sort of marriage even modern couples would envy. Professional and personal equals who respect and admire one another, the Bonners are also clearly comfortable in their roles as man and woman and are passionately, warmly attracted to one another.

When they find themselves representing opposing sides in a sensational trial, the issues that emerge in the case—a sordid domestic dispute involving a husband's infidelity and his wife's outraged response—soon stir the tranquil waters of the Bonner marriage. The trial and the film ask, *What are the rights of a husband? What are those of a wife? And are those rights equal, or are they not?* The sophisticated, well-educated Bonners are surprised to find troubling preconceptions lurking beneath the surface of even their warmly compatible, modern marriage of equals.

The great gift of the Libra marriage is the promise of real admiration and collaboration between two people who consider themselves equal. But like the Bonners—or, to use a real-life example, Bill and Hillary Clinton, who married with the Sun in Libra—no couple is safe from the clash of gender expectations or the most stereotypical sort of infidelity or other peccadilloes. If anything, these conflicts are even more troubling when they rear up in an otherwise sophisticated marriage full of mutual respect—because they are so completely unexpected.

The Libra Season

The Libra season begins at the autumnal equinox, when day and night are roughly equivalent in length, and lasts through harvest time until the third week in October. With deciduous trees changing color and a brisk bite entering the air, this is one of the most beautiful seasons of the year—appropriately for a month ruled by Venus, the goddess of beauty.

Libra's ruling planet is Venus, the Roman goddess of love and beauty, a symbol of feminine sensuality and pleasure. In myth, Venus married and gave birth, but diverted her attention to extramarital affairs and beauty treatments rather than domestic and caretaking concerns.

Astrological Libra is the sign associated with legal relationships including marriage, and its season is therefore considered a beneficial time to wed. The Sun is considered "weak" in the sign of Libra; appropriately, since the Sun symbolizes individual ego and Libra demands that we set the ego aside and cooperate with others.

How It Begins: The Libra Wedding

Of all signs, Libra is most likely to favor the nightmare contemporary wedding style of puffy chiffon, ribbons and bows, and lots and lots of pink—the Venus feminine archetype run amok! Less stereotypical Libra couples will favor an extremely tasteful approach, often with a delicate Asian flavor. You'll choose candid black and white photography instead of glossy posed wedding shots; exquisite food, including a tasteful fondant-draped cake; and formalwear that is simple, quiet, and stunningly elegant.

The sign of Libra has a strong connection with the western horizon, so a wedding at sunset, as the Sun disappears in the west, would be beautiful and appropriate. Music, so dear to the heart of Venus, plays an important role in your Libra wedding. Choose a string quartet, an a cappella vocal group, or a harpist to create a classic, romantic atmosphere.

Include an equal number of bridesmaids and groomsmen, please—nothing quirky or asymmetrical for a Libra wedding. Colors associated with Libra are ivory, pink/rose, and soft blue. For flowers, emphasize delicate, fragrant blooms such as the dahlia, tuberose, magnolia, or Asian lily. A few long-stemmed flowers wrapped in satin ribbon will make an elegant bouquet for the Venusian bride.

The Care and Feeding of Your Libra Marriage

THE PURPOSE OF A LIBRA MARRIAGE

If you're in a Libra marriage, it's because on some level you understood that you can be most effective in the world in **collaboration** with another person. Take a look at Bill and Hillary Clinton, for heaven's sake; those are two formidable people. But while they were smart and determined, it wasn't until they joined forces that they became a real presence in the public eye.

Your marriage exists to show the world at large that **together, you can achieve more than you can individually**. Mind you, the trick is to marry wisely—someone who is your match in smarts, looks, talent, drive, and ambition. Anyone less than an absolute equal is going to drag you down, and the whole of your marriage will quickly become less than the sum of its parts.

WHAT THE LIBRA MARRIAGE NEEDS

In a word, **togetherness**. You value having a partner to act as the sounding board for your individual dreams and ideas. By constantly monitoring yourself against your partner, you gain a clear understanding of who you are. The constant mirroring of your spouse increases self-awareness for you both and strengthens you as you confront your weaknesses and test your strengths.

SOURCES OF FRICTION

Not everyone is a team player. The Aries, Leo, Sagittarius, or Capricorn individual is going to need to be acknowledged, at least in public, as the alpha dog in this marriage—first among equals, if you will—or things are going to get pretty strained. Leo political dynamos Bill Clinton and Barack Obama and Sagittarian film directors David Mamet and Steven Spielberg have all flourished in their Libra marriages. Each has a formidable spouse, yet retains top billing in public.

Behind the scenes, the distribution of power in your marriage is likely to be more equitable. But the delays and negotiations needed to reach consensus at every turn may require ongoing adjustment for the "lone wolf" personality.

The Libra Marriage Style

THE FACE YOU SHOW THE WORLD

You put your marriage first, before any other relationship or concern, and regardless of your problems or disappointments, you almost unfailingly present a united front in public. You approach each new situation in life by instinctively figuring out the best way to "spin" it—how to behave, which words to use, even how to dress to influence matters in your favor.

WHAT YOU OWN

To the extent possible, the financial goal of your marriage should be to achieve financial independence through judicious investments. You are tremendously talented at making other people rather wealthy, which is all good and well as long as you find a way to work the same magic for yourselves!

While you're working your way toward financial independence, you may find you're uniquely well suited to making money through activities that others find distasteful. Examples include work that brings you into close contact with life's unpleasant realities (estate law, plumbing, psychology, hospice care) or that is associated with with negative stereotypes (attorneys, dentists, funeral directors, politicians).

HOW YOU COMMUNICATE

You enjoy good, long, philosophical conversations, whether with each other or with friends, and you vastly prefer discussions of life's big mysteries to chitchat or idle gossip. Rather at odds with the polite, measured face you show the world, those who enter into a conversation with you soon find that you're capable of being funny, earthy, and irreverent.

You will enjoy living in neighborhoods that are culturally diverse, with interesting ethnic restaurants, a good library, and perhaps even a university nearby. You're fond of taking short, impromptu trips to relatively distant places, and pride yourselves on being able to exchange pleasantries in at least one language other than your native tongue.

HOW YOU LIVE

You are likely to work out of your home, or to have careers related to domestic or real estate concerns such as real estate broker, mortgage banker, or professional chef. Having a well-appointed, professional home office is very important for you; if at all possible, look for a property with a separate structure that can be used for seeing clients, or at least a room with a separate public entrance for this purpose.

Your choice of home leans toward the traditional, and you are drawn toward well-built, interesting architecture. You prefer clean, modern interiors without a lot of fuss or clutter, and will favor the "less is more" philosophy of furnishing, choosing fewer pieces of the finest quality over many cheaper bits of furniture.

You are somewhat less likely than other couples to do a lot of entertaining at home, with the exceptions being formal family dinners or business-related entertaining. Part of this might be due to a lack of space, as you find you are drawn to upscale urban areas where square footage is at a premium.

YOUR CHILDREN AND CREATIVE SPIRIT

You consider your children unique and brilliant—and who's to say you're wrong? You prefer a fairly hands-off approach to child rearing, setting strict limits and expectations but allowing your offspring to find their own way within those parameters. You are more likely than many couples to befriend young people, whether in a parental or mentorship role. If you don't have children of your own, you will quickly attain the status of "cool aunt and uncle" among your nieces and nephews.

You are a uniquely creative couple. Libra is known for its keen appreciation of the arts, and you encourage one another to cultivate an assortment of creative endeavors. There will be plenty of music in your home, and you seem to have a flair for working artistically with electronic media, such as film or video. Your friends are often your creative collaborators and a source of inspiration.

YOUR WORK, HEALTH, AND DAILY ROUTINE

You are idealistic about the kinds of work you'd like to do, and encourage each other to pursue work that makes a difference. You are enthusiastic volunteers and involve others in various worthy causes, particularly those related to peace and the relief of human illness, poverty, and famine. Wise management of your resources may allow you to retire early to pursue your humanitarian and philanthropic interests full-time.

You develop a daily routine that's highly flexible, and because you have a hard time saying no, you try to pack an awful lot into any given day. This is commendable, but it can also lead to chronic lateness and feeling run-down, resulting in persistent illnesses such as infections and colds. Encourage one another to make time for rest and relaxation; if you don't safeguard your health, there is little you can do to help others. You needn't become slaves to the clock, but make a commitment to eating regular meals, paying your bills on time, and getting plenty of rest. Carrying the weight of the world is exhausting.

YOUR FRIENDS AND FOES

Because you present an image of sweet, tranquil togetherness, the wild, headstrong troublemakers of the world are magnetically drawn into your orbit. You enjoy their reckless energy and watch in awe as they take up the sword against any foe, real or imagined. The true friends among them will fight battles just as passionately on your behalf.

But those who are not true friends—or who are, in fact, your enemies—will attack you openly and may initially leave you bleeding. It's a truth that our enemies are in a position to be our most powerful friends, because they reveal both our strengths and our weaknesses. Your rash, willful enemies reveal your tactical prowess and ability to win others to your cause by dint of charm and without bloodshed. They also teach you that there are moments in life when you have no choice but to remove your dagger from its sheath and deal your enemies a mortal blow.

WHAT YOU SHARE

You are extremely comfortable with one another and quite secure in your relationship. However, you are unlikely to spend much time probing life's great mysteries together, and the intimate side of your relationship—while highly enjoyable and quite satisfying—tends not to be all-consuming.

Something about your marital chemistry attracts financial extremes; you fluctuate between great wealth and rather tenuous financial circumstances. You favor investments that seem solid and secure, such as bonds, real estate, and equities, but while you don't tend to lose much money with this strategy, it can be a difficult tactic for achieving financial independence.

WHAT YOU BELIEVE

You believe in facts and ideas, in asking questions and in training the intellect. You believe in maintaining an attitude of healthy skepticism toward all beliefs, an attitude that does little to endear you to those with strong convictions.

This is not to suggest that you aren't interested in religion or philosophy; in fact, you find nothing else as fascinating as what other people believe to be true about life. Even if you are individually devout, however, your marriage will encourage you to examine your beliefs, your faith, the things you know, and the customs of your culture.

YOUR CONTRIBUTION TO THE WORLD

Your approach to the world of business is to make it a family affair. You are almost certainly in the same line of work, and it's likely that you'll groom your children to take their place in that world.

Your private lives, including the most sensitive details, are likely to be highly influential in public perceptions of your marriage. First Lady Betty Ford's battles with alcoholism and addiction to painkillers were eventually made public and led to the founding of the Betty Ford clinic for substance abuse recovery. President Bill Clinton's philandering led to scandal and impeachment. The message is not that you should demand perfection of yourselves, or of one another; the truth is, every person and every marriage has personal matters that they would prefer to keep private. However, it seems to be your path to live as honorably as you know how and to try to use your personal setbacks to create structural changes in society that help others.

YOUR PLACE IN SOCIETY

It is not an exaggeration to say that your friends are the key to your success. You count among your social set the richest, most famous, most magnetic and glittering friends possible. Although you do not choose them for these qualities—in fact, you adore their humor, playfulness, and zest for living—it would be disingenuous to say that your connections with them are not helpful to you in pursuing your goals together.

Together, you have a gift for befriending perfect strangers and putting them at ease. Nearly everyone you meet finds that they can identify with you. Indeed, you are particularly charismatic when you find a video camera trained on you or a microphone thrust in your faces. Perhaps that's why so many politicians seem to gravitate toward Libra marriages!

YOUR PRIVATE SANCTUARY

The face you show the world is a smooth, smiling mask that completely obscures the massive worry and stress behind the scenes. But going through life negotiating, flattering, and doing your best to get along with everyone you meet is an extremely demanding and draining way to live. The standards you set for yourselves are high, and reaching them puts a burden on your bodies, minds, and spirits.

Behind the closed doors of your marriage, there is constant study, rehearsal, and polishing. It takes a lot of hard work to cultivate the illusion of effortlessness that you show the world. You are extremely guarded about your quiet time; you don't sleep or rest well, and you need time to yourselves in order to relax and prepare for everyday life—a life of shining your shoes, polishing your teeth, and setting out into the world with smiles on your faces, determined to win the hearts and minds of everyone you meet.

The Scorpio Marriage
(OCTOBER 24–NOVEMBER 22)

Famous Sun-in-Scorpio Marriages

Carly Simon and James Taylor (Nov. 3)
Frank Sinatra and Ava Gardner (Nov. 7)
Queen Elizabeth II and Prince Philip (Nov. 20)
Bruce Willis and Demi Moore (Nov. 21)

❧

Although she married only once and the marriage didn't last long, actress Katherine Hepburn made a fine career of portraying some of film's most intriguing wives. In films as varied as *Adam's Rib*, *Guess Who's Coming to Dinner*, and *On Golden Pond*, Hepburn specialized in playing spunky, headstrong women married to crusty, opinionated men who matched her peppery spirit.

My very favorite of Hepburn's onscreen marriages was her Eleanor of Aquitaine to Peter O'Toole's Henry II in *The Lion in Winter*. O'Toole's Henry is a handsome, swaggering lion of a king, ruthless and charismatic. After decades of marriage to Eleanor, a French queen who brought to her marriage a fortune in personal assets and the gift of mesmerizing men, Henry has decided to imprison his wife because "you led too many civil wars against me" ("And I damn near won the last one!" she retorts). The film's plot revolves around Henry and Eleanor's dispute over which of their sons will inherit Henry's crown. Henry favors weak and childish John; Eleanor, the bloodthirsty Richard. It is the Christmas season, and Eleanor has been released from prison to spend the holidays with her family. But the spirit that prevails over the royal household is hardly one of warm reconciliation. Over the course of the film, Henry and Eleanor spar and plot like world-class swordsmen, manipulating each other and their sons with breathtaking skill and ruthlessness.

But although Henry has imprisoned his wife and is bedding a young noblewoman whom Eleanor raised—and although Eleanor has proven she will stop at nothing to have her way—it's obvious the two are enthralled by one another. During a quiet intermission in their hostilities, reminiscing about the early days of their marriage, Eleanor gives Henry an adoring sidelong look. "You're still a marvel of a man," she tells him. "And you," Henry replies, "are my lady."

The Scorpio marriage is born in a season with all the fierce passion and loyalty—and yes, possibly some of the intrigue—of Henry and Eleanor's union. You will not always be friends; that is the truth of intimate relationships. You will not even, perhaps, always be kind to one another. But you will never, ever lose the fascination that first drew you together.

The Scorpio Season

The Sun is in Scorpio in late October and the first few weeks of November. It's not a terribly popular time of year for weddings in the Northern Hemisphere, where the weather is turning cool. Generally speaking, it's not the blushing young bride and groom in the first bloom of romantic love who marry in Scorpio. It is a darker, colder season in the waning cycle of the year, and it demands a particular quality of commitment— and the ability to look life, and marriage, squarely in the eye.

In myth, Scorpio corresponds to Mars, the god of war, and to Hades (Pluto), god of the underworld. Scorpio is the astrological symbol for death and endings, of the transformation of energy from one form to another. The stark imagery of Scorpio, with its reminders of mortality and the dark night of the soul, is reflected in the celebrations of the Scorpio season: Halloween, with its origins in the pagan celebration of Samhain; the Mexican Día de los Muertos (Day of the Dead); and Veterans Day (U.S.), when war veterans (reflecting Scorpio's traditional planetary rulership by Mars, the planet of war) are honored.

Individuals born with the Sun in Scorpio are possessed of formidable will power and the ability to probe beneath the surface of any situation and quickly apprehend the truth. The intense, powerful, and strategic qualities of Scorpio are best suited to a couple who share a deep sense of purpose—a determination to succeed and endure. If you share these qualities, the Scorpio marriage can be one of great loyalty, passion, and longevity.

How It Begins: The Scorpio Wedding

The Scorpio wedding must, above all, acknowledge and honor the spirit of the season, the implication that everything eventually comes to an end. How to honor such a grim prognosis in a celebration of love and commitment?

First of all, this is not an appropriate season for a traditional white-and-pastel extravaganza filled with lush roses and tulle. Some note of mystery or controversy usually accompanies the Scorpio wedding—a pregnant bride, in-laws at war, obsessed ex-partners who crash the party. Nothing looks sillier than gothic drama played against a backdrop of organza and tea roses; the Scorpio wedding must be as bold and arresting as the sign itself. This wedding season demands a couple who want to shake up their family and friends with an outrageous theme, hide from the matrimonial spotlight altogether and elope, or quietly exchange vows before a small dinner party with close friends.

Whatever the venue, this is no time for subtle pinks and soft blues ... pull out the colors of late autumn: dark shades of red, burnt orange, poison green, even some black. If you crave a conventional church ceremony, honor Scorpio's intensity with an intimate, candlelit evening ceremony, with attendants dressed in chic basic black and the bride in crimson.

The flowers should be exotic, sculptural, and striking in color and fragrance, such as amaranth (also called "love lies bleeding"), amaryllis (belladonna lily), kniphofia (red hot poker), hibiscus, orchids, gardenias, dahlias, and lilies. Scatter pomegranates, sacred to Pluto, on tables, mantels, or altars, and use plenty of candles or luminarias for lighting.

The Care and Feeding of Your Scorpio Marriage

THE PURPOSE OF A SCORPIO MARRIAGE

A marriage born in the Scorpio season exists to **celebrate life's mysteries**—and its grim ironies. A woman's father dies when she is seven months pregnant with her first child; a favorite colleague's untimely death leads to your promotion; your best friend gets in a car accident on the way to your wedding. It all sounds like simple bad luck, but to Scorpio—trained to look below the surface and to find the subtle connections that bind all things together—there is a pattern at work. Good things, by nature's law of balance, must at some point be answered by bad things, and vice-versa.

Astrologer and writer Dana Gerhardt writes,

> In Scorpio's month, the answer is simply to Enter the Mystery.
> We do not have to recite elaborate mantras or appeal for divine
> assistance with specially colored candles. To enter the mystery
> requires only that we acknowledge there are things we just don't
> know. Instead of chasing thoughts around, like running after
> leaves fluttering in the wind, let's just sit with what is. Sit with the
> sentence "I don't know." Notice the strange comfort of abandon-
> ing the mind's attempt to understand and control. Something
> in the body rises in awareness. Unafraid of what is, it welcomes
> mystery with a kind of clarity and calm.*

Into each life, and each marriage, a little rain must fall. There is a
very good reason why the vows we recite with such tender faith and
breathlessness on our wedding day contain such scary dichotomies—
richer or poorer, better or worse, in sickness or in health—it's because
life itself contains them. In the Scorpio marriage, you don't fool yourselves into thinking you have a secret formula for outwitting life's
tough times. You are willing to sit with the mystery, and to admit, "We
don't know what's coming next."

---

* From "Enter the Mystery" by Dana Gerhardt. Published at MoonCircles.com, November 2006.

WHAT THE SCORPIO MARRIAGE NEEDS

To feel your Scorpio marriage is a success, you need to feel really alive—even when you'd rather not feel anything at all. You're the type of couple who has passionate arguments and enjoys the process of making up afterward. You are likely to feel your relationship is fated and that you were brought together by the forces of destiny; this may or may not be true, but you certainly feel that it is. Your great horror would be to settle into a marriage that is stable, unchanging, and passive.

The Scorpio marriage also thrives on total honesty. There is no room at all in this relationship for the slightest hint of insincerity, subterfuge, manipulation, or little white lies; Scorpio simply won't stand for it. Where there is dishonesty, Scorpio cannot feel trust, and trust is what is required for Scorpio to fully surrender to total commitment and intimacy.

SOURCES OF FRICTION

In real life, sometimes we feel like taking the intensity down just a notch. Every now and then, eating a chicken potpie in front of the television sounds like exactly what we want to do on a rainy fall evening. Does *every* night have to feature the drama, the *Sturm und Drang*, of arguments and makeup sex? Does *every* conversation need to be quite so heavy? How about a little chitchat in there to lighten things up?

The first weeks of a relationship, when the sexual thrall is at its peak, are thrilling—but do you want to spend every day of the rest of your lives in that state of romantic intoxication? If you're a pretty intense person by nature, well then, sure. And if on the other end of the scale you're an extremely mellow and down-to-earth person and nothing fazes you, then yeah, the Scorpio marriage might inject a welcome note of excitement into your life. But for those who fall somewhere in between (say, an Aries or Leo—passionate, but less introspective), the intensity level of the Scorpio marriage can be a little wearing at times.

The Scorpio Marriage Style

THE FACE YOU SHOW THE WORLD

The Scorpio marriage values intimate connections above all else. You evaluate each new acquaintance and every new situation that comes your way based on the honesty and integrity you find there. If these are lacking, you move on quickly; but if you like what you see, you commit yourselves fully.

WHAT YOU OWN

You enjoy money as much as the next couple, but you are open-handed with what you have because you're usually optimistic that there is plenty more where that came from. You're willing to spend money on education, because you realize your mind is your very best natural resource. You're also quite happy to invest in travel … the more exotic the destination, the better.

Sources of income that are especially lucrative for the two of you include publishing, teaching, the travel industry, and to a certain extent, law. You are especially likely to do some portion of your work from home, or to make home/real estate/domestic concerns the focus of your work. For instance, you might have a home-based business that provides escrow services, or you might publish e-books about cooking.

HOW YOU COMMUNICATE

You may not be terribly chatty with one another, preferring conversations that have a practical point to those that are purely recreational. This may take some adjustment if either of you enjoys gossip and chitchat, but silence doesn't necessarily mean you're not communicating. Interestingly, you may have careers that involve communication, in fields such as public relations, law, or publishing. In fact, if you work together, you are likely to use your profession as a way of communicating about personal matters.

If you do find you have trouble communicating with one another, at least you are willing to be serious and task-oriented about resolving the problem. You are one of the few couples who ask for advice and then actually *take* the advice—especially if you paid for it!

You are also exceptionally good at giving advice, and may find that young people in your life are drawn to your home for guidance and counsel. For one thing, you're good at shutting up and letting other people do the talking, and for another, people sense—correctly—that you can be trusted with a secret.

HOW YOU LIVE

For a couple who are essentially grounded and stable, you certainly have a tendency to move around a lot. You might find it challenging to live in one place for more than a few years at a time; at the very least, you'll keep tinkering with your house, renovating, refurbishing, and moving things around. Your home is aglow and abuzz with technology—plenty of computers, machines, gadgets, and entertainment equipment. You are "at home" with technology, and at least one of you is a whiz whom friends call upon to tame troublesome machines.

Speaking of friends, they tend to accumulate in your home—your house is the gathering place for parties, celebrations, and watching the Academy Awards or Super Bowl on television. On the other hand, you tend to be fairly independent from your families, usually living far enough away to discourage spontaneous visits, though you are likely to be on friendly terms with family members. In many ways, your friends—who have been allowed into your lives based on loyalty and trustworthiness rather than accidents of birth—are your true family.

YOUR CHILDREN AND CREATIVE SPIRIT

If you have children, you will let them know that they are loved unconditionally. You also tend to be fairly permissive parents, allowing them independence at a relatively early age and relying on your ability to "read" your kids and elicit the truth from them in order to keep them in line.

If you don't have children, your creative pursuits will take center stage in your lives. Your home will be filled with artwork, your musician friends will congregate for jam sessions in your living room, and if you can manage it, there will be a studio for pottery, writing, or woodworking. Your creative work is often where you express your most cherished beliefs, and is an important way of experiencing and sharing your spirituality.

YOUR WORK, HEALTH, AND DAILY ROUTINE

You are hard workers, always in a hurry, and probably don't take care of yourselves as well as you should. Lots of physical exercise is the most important key to your continued good health—in particular competitive sports—but you also bring out one another's daring sides and may gamble any gains in health for the thrill of risk-taking.

You may find that you are impatient with details and unwilling to compromise in your work. You can't countenance close supervision and are happiest as free agents or in work that requires a lot of independent judgment and allows you to move at your own pace.

YOUR FRIENDS AND FOES

Your friends exhibit the best qualities of Taurus, your opposite sign: patient, easy-going, and immune to shock. Your friends are people you can really depend upon—and that's how you see your marriage partner too, as dependable if sometimes a bit stubborn. From you, your friends can vicariously experience the passion, drama, and spice of a marriage that is less an institution than a force of nature.

Your foes, on the other hand, exhibit the least attractive Taurus traits, such as a closed mind. The Scorpio marriage is interested in what goes on underneath the surface in life—the magic and invisible forces that make life rich and fascinating. Anyone who dismisses the mystical aspects of existence out of hand is not a person who will add much to your enjoyment of life!

WHAT YOU SHARE

Communication is the key to your intimacy. Without a meeting of the minds, your sexual relationship will suffer. Generally you're willing to talk about the darkest corners of your past, your minds, and your relationship—literally no topic is off limits!

Money and investments interest you as topics of conversation too, and you're pretty astute about these matters. You generally have several income streams, and in fact do best when you rely on multiple sources of income rather than focusing on just one. Financial analysts overwhelmingly recommend diversifying your investments, and since that is your instinctive approach, you are likely to build a very fine portfolio.

WHAT YOU BELIEVE

You believe in the importance of family and a sense of place. Perhaps because you spend so much of your lives exploring the dark and unsettling dimensions of the human experience, you cling to many of the traditions, customs, and beliefs that were the underpinning of your early lives. Oddly, though, you might move fairly often. You have a strong reaction to foreign influences in your home ... foreign guests, foreign food, artwork and music from other cultures. You either love what is foreign or hate it, and are not shy about letting the world know where you stand!

It's also quite likely that one or both of you has some kind of education or credentials related to homes, such as a real estate license, mortgage brokerage license, or food service or inspection license. You might even teach something related to these fields. You are particularly likely to own property in a country other than your country of birth at some point, most likely a vacation home. While you may not travel often, when you do, you want to feel at home.

YOUR CONTRIBUTION TO THE WORLD

You're intensely private in your personal lives, but in your careers you stand out and let yourselves be noticed. Careers in entertainment or a related field are quite likely. You shine in public and seem very outgoing, but are very private about inviting others into your inner circle. Your pizzazz and style make yours the kind of marriage people look up to; you always appear to be having a good time, and yet you project a certain dignity and royal bearing that inspires respect.

The public side of your relationship may also be a contentious area of your marriage if either of you is very reclusive or finds it difficult to share the spotlight. The Scorpio marriage works only when you are in agreement about the public face of the marriage. In fact, one of the sure ways to sabotage your marriage is to indulge in a public indiscretion and embarrass your partner.

YOUR PLACE IN SOCIETY

You care strongly about a number of important issues, but you're not joiners, as a rule. Still, you can be persuaded to become involved with associations that support causes dear to your hearts, because you find it very gratifying to help others who are in need.

You are a bit preoccupied with health, especially concerns that you will experience serious health problems in old age. Allow these concerns to inspire you to practice good health maintenance routines in the present, especially a healthy diet, and trust that you are doing all you can to safeguard your future health. You are most vulnerable to illnesses related to stress and worry, such as digestive problems and skin problems, so worrying about your future health is a prescription for creating many of the problems you fear!

YOUR PRIVATE SANCTUARY

As a couple, you are much more romantic and artistically refined than most people guess. Your best-kept secret, though—one you will go to any lengths to protect—is that you're a lot more concerned about getting along with other people than you seem. You bring out a "testing" spirit in one another, and your occasional mind games in interacting with other people are nothing more than a way of finding out whether they can be trusted. You'd rather not do this; in fact, you'd rather be lovers, not fighters, and give everyone the benefit of the doubt. It's simply not your style.

You're also quite protective of the details of your married life. For married couples in the public eye, the prying of media and fans for information about your marriage is truly painful. Your marriage is absolutely sacred to you, and not even your closest friends really appreciate the strength of the bond you share.

The Sagittarius Marriage

(NOV. 23–DEC. 21)

Famous Sun-in-Sagittarius Marriages

Desi Arnaz and Lucille Ball (Nov. 30)
Garson Kanin and Ruth Gordon (Dec. 2)
Diana Krall and Elvis Costello (Dec. 5)
Georgia O'Keeffe and Alfred Stieglitz (Dec. 11)

❧

One of the most popular television series of all time, *I Love Lucy*, was a situation comedy chronicling the daffy adventures of a clownish redhead named Lucy Ricardo and her Cuban bandleader husband, Ricky. The Ricardos were portrayed by real-life couple Desi Arnaz and Lucille Ball, who were married when the Sun was in Sagittarius.

I Love Lucy portrayed the conflict and humor of an intercultural marriage (Desi Arnaz as Ricky speaks in a heavy Cuban accent and when frustrated lapses into rapid-fire Spanish) with classic, Sagittarian physical comedy. The real-life Arnaz/Ball marriage was not quite as good-natured as the Ricardos', marred by Arnaz's infidelity and Ball's overbearing nature. But the real-life marriage was also a good deal more fascinating than the fictional one. Far from the ditzy housewife she portrayed on television, Lucille Ball was one of the most powerful and savvy businesswomen in Hollywood. And more than just a smooth, charming crooner, Desi Arnaz was a dazzling innovator in television production. Together, they literally changed the way television programming was produced and distributed.

Traditional astrologers associated Sagittarius with "foreigners," and those who marry with the Sun in this sign are likely to have significant differences in background or outlook. Whether you come from different countries, religions, or socioeconomic backgrounds, or simply have very different temperaments, you are foreign and fascinating to one another. From this clash of cultures can come unexpected vision and inspiration. Your Sagittarius marriage stimulates the parts of your individual personalities that are always seeking new challenges, visions, and frontiers. You'll incite one another to dream big dreams, and to never say never. You may not change the face of television, but it's certain the world will grow bigger for both of you because you are together.

The Sagittarius Season

The Sun is in Sagittarius from the last part of November through the first few weeks in December; in the Northern Hemisphere, it's one of the bleakest, chilliest seasons of the year. In the United States, the festive observance of Thanksgiving takes place on the last Thursday of November, during Sagittarius's season. And of course, in many countries the entire month of December is given over to jovial—even excessive—preparations for the lavish winter holidays: Hanukkah, Christmas, Solstice, and Kwanzaa.

Blessed with more vision and confidence than its fire-sign brethren Aries and Leo, Sagittarius is ruled by Jupiter (Zeus), the king of the gods. With a pedigree like that, we can hardly blame Sagittarius for thinking big. Mythical Zeus was popular with the ladies, his kingly status making him hard to resist. He was not, however, constant in love; though infidelity is far from fated for the Sagittarius marriage, Zeus's wandering eye can cause trouble for inconstant or highly jealous partners.

Impatient with details, the astrological Sagittarius takes a long view and just plain dreams bigger than other people. The Sagittarius couple is not simply pioneering like the Aries couple, not simply motivated by creative passions like the Leo couple; rather, you think in terms of total world domination and will never feel happy with human-scale ambitions and achievements. For those who marry during the Sagittarius season, the sky's the limit—and nothing less than the whole sky will do.

How It Begins: The Sagittarius Wedding

It bears repeating: Sagittarius is not fond of details. If one or the other of you is strongly influenced by Gemini or Virgo, you may be a little more interested in booking a caterer and registering for a china pattern. But generally, Sagittarius favors a more spontaneous approach to ceremony, which is fortunate since the frenetic pace of the holiday season can present logistic challenges for a complicated wedding.

Sagittarius, along with Taurus and Virgo, has a profound appreciation for nature, so if you live in a warm climate, consider holding your wedding outdoors, preferably in a place with some hint of wilderness about it—in the mountains, at the edge of a forest, on the beach. Along with Pisces, Sagittarius enjoys borrowing ceremonial elements from other cultures. Native American, Indian, or African cultural elements find their way into your wedding via native clothing, music, or rituals.

The colors of Sagittarius are the hues of Mardi Gras: purple, yellow, and green. In ancient times, purple, as one of the most difficult shades to achieve, was reserved for royalty, so it is a fitting color for a "royal" Sagittarius wedding.

Sagittarius is less interested in flowers than in greenery, so use a lot of beautiful foliage, such as ivy, in your bouquets and arrangements. Sagittarius flowers include carnations and irises, but consider adorning church pews, chairs, altars, mantelpieces, and banquet tables with great swags of evergreen studded with pine cones, holly with bright berries, and mistletoe and rosemary. All of these evoke the Sagittarian love of nature and are appropriate for late November and December.

The Care and Feeding of Your Sagittarius Marriage

THE PURPOSE OF A SAGITTARIUS MARRIAGE

The Sagittarius marriage has an evolutionary urge to **explore**, and exploration requires the unshakable conviction that there is something out there waiting to be found. Therefore, the Sagittarius marriage does not promote open-mindedness; rather, it nurtures the tremendous confidence in your own beliefs and opinions that is required to venture together into uncharted territory.

WHAT THE SAGITTARIUS MARRIAGE NEEDS

Above all, you need shared **vision**. Your journey together requires that you encourage each other to trust your individual and collective visions, and to move toward them with passion and conviction. Without such an overarching inspiration to guide you, you can become lazy about venturing outside your intellectual comfort zone.

SOURCES OF FRICTION

Ever known a couple who are so sure they're right about everything that you want to throttle them—even when you agree with their opinions? Don't be that couple! Because you are learning to trust your own beliefs and visions, you are sometimes insensitive to the fact that others may have completely different ways of seeing the world. If taken to extremes, this insensitivity can snowball into arrogance, costing you friendships and goodwill. Fortunately, this is completely avoidable. You are right to build each other's confidence in the truth and rightness of your individual beliefs and visions, but take care not to impose those beliefs on each other, much less on the rest of the world.

The Sagittarius Marriage Style

THE FACE YOU SHOW THE WORLD

Optimistic, sometimes to a fault; candid, often to the point of tactlessness; exuberant, occasionally to lampshade-on-the-head extremes. You're a couple who will nearly always meet life with a jaunty grin and the unshakable sense that "nothing is *that* bad." This almost reckless naïveté can get you into trouble from time to time—you may trust the wrong people, make mistakes with your investments, or fall victim to con artists' scams. Overall, though, yours is a happy way to go through life, believing the best about each other, the people around you, and the future you share.

WHAT YOU OWN

A marriage as optimistic and ebullient as yours needs some kind of weight to pull you down to earth; and for the two of you, that ballast is likely to be money. You do not have the luxury of taking a casual approach to the financial side of life; unless you are prepared to behave with great maturity, seriousness, and strategy in this area of your marriage, you are likely to encounter a steady stream of financial obstacles.

If you are willing to curb your tendency toward excess and approach your resources in a businesslike matter, though, you can achieve extraordinary success. Consider Desi Arnaz and Lucille Ball, who together launched Desilu, a highly successful television studio with a pioneering approach to producing television shows.

HOW YOU COMMUNICATE

Simply put, you make one another smarter. By sharpening your wits with one another, and through the unique situations, friends, and ideas that are drawn to you, you develop instincts and insights that are nothing short of revolutionary. Together, you have a talent of presenting information and ideas in a way that is startlingly new and very exciting.

You have the potential to be very comfortable with technology, and are likely "early adopters" who are comfortable using every form of electric gadget. You believe that using technology actually trains you to be smarter, and there may be something to that. In any event, you don't need to ask ten-year-olds to program your television recorder for you—you're more than capable of figuring it out on your own.

HOW YOU LIVE

You'll live near the water if you can, and if you can't, you'll have a swimming pool, fountain, or aquarium. At the very least, incorporate the colors and motifs of the ocean into your décor. Music, artwork, and photography play an important part in your home life, and musical instruments, artwork, and photos abound.

Your home is your sanctuary, and you prefer a quiet and soothing atmosphere. Even if you are not religious people, sacred icons often show up in your home: novena candles, statues of the Buddha, makeshift altars with incense and pictures of departed family members.

In the outside world, you are each expressive, even extroverted, but within your home, the atmosphere is tranquil and healing.

YOUR CHILDREN AND CREATIVE SPIRIT

Yours is among the most creative marriages—not because you have more creative ideas (although you have more than the average), but because you are utterly fearless in pursuing them. Some may envy what they perceive as your luck and talent, but you know that while you possess your share of these, your success is really due to brawn and determination. You simply refuse to be told you can't do anything that you want to do.

Your children are often pulled into your creative sphere as well. Consider young Desi Arnaz Jr., whose real-life birth was written into an *I Love Lucy* story line and who later went into the family business—acting. Even if they don't follow you into your creative endeavors (and any children of yours are certain to be very strong-willed) they are sure to inspire yours, and to have courageous, entrepreneurial dreams of their own.

YOUR WORK, HEALTH, AND DAILY ROUTINE

Together you develop a daily routine that is comfortable and predictable, which promotes stable health and provides a supportive environment for pursuing your work. If there is a flaw in your daily habits, it is that the same adherence to routine that serves you so well can become toxic if bad habits become part of the routine.

The biggest threats to your health are overindulgence in drink and rich foods. You enjoy a good meal, and the natural ebullience you share makes it difficult for you to resist ordering another round of appetizers and another bottle of wine for the table. Add to this the fact that you resist exercise routines—preferring to get exercise as a natural part of performing everyday tasks, which is fine unless your everyday tasks are sedentary—and you have a potential recipe for excess weight and sluggish metabolisms.

YOUR FRIENDS AND FOES

Because you carry yourselves with such confidence, you are a magnet for people who have many ideas but few convictions. These are people who like being told what to do and believe, and it is difficult for you to resist telling them! You are apt to attract trickster types who entice you away from your dreams, or even from your exclusive commitment to one another.

Your closest friendships are likely to be based on intellectual compatibility rather than deep emotional connections. You enjoy bright, curious people who are fantastic conversationalists, and they make excellent friends for you, as they aren't afraid to question your wisdom and keep you from becoming too complacent and too insular in your thinking.

WHAT YOU SHARE

While you are intrepid in most areas of your marriage, you are naturally conservative but adept at managing your investments, debt, and shared resources. If you have a weakness in this area, it is that your emotional needs and your desire for security can sometimes override practical advice that could increase your shared wealth.

A sense of security in your marriage is also the key to your sexual compatibility and happiness. You are particularly tender, nurturing, and sensitive in your intimate moments, but are also vulnerable to problems resulting from unresolved emotional issues. It can be a bit difficult for you to talk as frankly about your sex life as about other areas of your marriage, because it's an area of great vulnerability for you both. This should become easier over time, provided you build up a sense of trust and security in all parts of your marriage.

WHAT YOU BELIEVE

Your marriage revolves around the world of philosophy, education, travel, and big ideas. Your creative vision takes you all over the world, whether literally or through the magic of media, and tends to draw on influences from other cultures and traditions as well.

Your marriage will tend to encourage you to further your education, showing you the weak spots in your knowledge or simply guiding you toward subjects that interest you deeply. Your marriage gives you additional confidence and magnetism that make you comfortable with the performance aspects of teaching. Showmanship combined with a love of ideas makes you natural teachers and may well lead you into careers as educators.

YOUR CONTRIBUTION TO THE WORLD

Perhaps because you are outgoing and love to laugh, people make the mistake of underestimating your ambition and business acumen—but this can work to your advantage. You're often perceived as worker bees and not moguls. And workers you are; your hands-on approach and attention to detail in your business enterprises give you an edge, both in the technical aspects of the work you do and in your approach to being in business.

You quickly acquire a reputation as perfectionists and "fixers" in anything you do. Regardless of the specific careers you pursue, you encourage each other in the direction of quality and integrity. Others may, in fact, be intimidated by your level of craftsmanship and daunted by the punishing standards to which you hold yourselves. Be mindful that your standards should be applied only to you and always appropriate to what you hope to achieve in the world; you should avoid harsh criticisms of others who do not share the standards you've set for yourselves.

YOUR PLACE IN SOCIETY

Probably, you began your relationship as friends, and that friendship remains the cornerstone of your marriage. Your friends are also a vital component of how successful you feel in your relationship; if you fail to develop friendships together, as opposed to making friends on your own and sharing them with one another, you will always feel as though there is something lacking in your relationship.

In planning for the future, your blind spot is in refusing to envision a scenario that doesn't include you both. This is sweet and romantic, but ignores important realities: it's likely that one of you will spend at least a portion of his or her life as a widow or widower. The best way to ensure the protective influence of your relationship after one of you is gone is to prepare a contingency plan that cares for the financial, physical, and companionship needs of the partner who is left behind.

YOUR PRIVATE SANCTUARY

On the face of it, you are a happy, funny, uncomplicated couple. And then someone crosses you and finds out in a hurry that you can be deadly adversaries. Your cheerful, upbeat demeanors may mask deep unhappiness in your individual pasts; perhaps you've seen something of life's saddest and most disappointing possibilities, and it's made you a little bit distrustful.

"You're only as sick as your secrets," as the saying goes, and the two of you have a lot of secrets. You've been through experiences that have demonstrated to you the prudence of not revealing too much of yourselves. So others may sometimes have the frustrating sense that they can't quite get close to you—that you know much more about them than they will ever know about you. In most cases, that's absolutely true. With each other, though, within the private walls of your marriage sanctuary, you feel safe enough to reveal every fear and share your darkest emotions. There is a deep bond between you that is much more profound than the upbeat façade you share with the world, a fierce protectiveness and trust that keeps you connected while you reach for the stars.

The Capricorn Marriage

(DECEMBER 22–JANUARY 20)

Famous Sun-in-Capricorn Marriages

Tom Cruise and Nicole Kidman (December 24)
Will Smith and Jada Pinkett Smith (December 31)
Bill and Melinda Gates (January 1)
George H. W. and Barbara Bush (January 6)

❧❧❧

$\mathcal{C}$apricorn is one of the "parental" signs, playing patriarch to Cancer's nurturing matriarch. In counterpoint to Cancer's emphasis on the nurturing of a single, family unit, Capricorn is a worldly sign, determined to enlarge its sphere of influence well beyond the boundaries of one small household. A couple that enters into a Capricorn marriage will never feel as if they are reaching their potential until they have reached a position of philanthropic influence. Capricorn is not satisfied with building one family, but it rather likes the idea of building a family *name*—a dynasty of influence and achievement that will outlast any single nuclear family unit.

You may not perpetuate a political dynasty, like George H. W. and Barbara Bush. Few are in a financial position to create charitable foundations on the scale of the Bill and Melinda Gates Foundation. You may not adopt children, like Tom Cruise and Nicole Kidman. But if you marry with the Sun in Capricorn, you will find a way to build your legacy.

My mother's sister and her husband were married on Christmas Day. They didn't leave a lot of money behind when they died, and they didn't have names you would recognize, yet they left a legacy of caring and philanthropy that influenced a wide community. Theirs was a two-career marriage well before that concept was popular, and my aunt, a banker, received a promotion to branch manager and vice president in an era when women rarely attained such influential positions. But they were compassionate, generous people whose two children often found themselves sharing their bunk beds with disadvantaged waifs, and my aunt was closely involved with a charitable organization that helped women escape from domestic violence. I benefited personally from their generosity. After my father died suddenly, we moved across country and lived for several years with my aunt, uncle, and cousins. Until they died, I considered them my "second parents."

The Capricorn Season

The Sun is in Capricorn from the winter solstice (December 21) through late January—the coldest and least hospitable weather of the year. On the other hand, with its many national holidays and vacations from school and work, it's a rather convenient time to marry. Cozy nuptials next to the familial hearth, a church decked with swags of evergreen and lit with candles, a quiet blanket of snow outside . . . sort of romantic, really, as long as you don't pine for a sleeveless gown and an outdoor wedding.

January is named for the Roman god Janus, the ruler of doorways and thresholds, including the threshold between the old year and the new. Janus symbolized change and transition and was worshipped at harvest and planting seasons, as well as beginnings—such as marriage.

Astrologically, the Capricorn season has worldly and practical connotations that don't exactly jibe with modern notions of romantic love and "happily ever after." Capricorn, ruled by stern Saturn, is considered a symbol of tough pragmatism and ambition, of grownups with real-world concerns. Like Scrooge, Capricorn's story is one of balancing worldly ambition with the tender world of the heart, home, and family. When you walk down the aisle during the Capricorn season, you may be dearly in love—but what will keep you together is what you build together.

How It Begins: The Capricorn Wedding

Serious and conservative, Capricorn wants a *tasteful* wedding. Money can be spent, but it should reflect an appreciation for quality and functionality. The venue will be chosen primarily for practical reasons (a friend claims her husband chose late December for their wedding because the church would already be decorated for Christmas—thus saving money on flowers!), and perhaps with a nod to tradition, such as the family manse or church.

Capricorn is not known for wild partying, but it *is* an earth sign after all, and it enjoys earthly pleasures like good food and good liquor. That's *good* liquor, mind you. And *quality* food. A buffet-style reception will earn you a sniff and a raised eyebrow from your patron sign: as far as Capricorn is considered, one *sits* at dinner and is *served* one's meal—preferably on good china. Capricorn has a deep respect for history, so invite traditional touches into your ceremony: the grandmother's ring, the "giving away" of the bride. The vows and service will be dignified; customization will be minimal. Classical music is favored over rehashed folk tunes.

Dignified, subdued shades such as forest green, black, charcoal gray, or indigo blue are the best choices for a Capricorn wedding. The Capricorn bride is one of the few who will almost never drape her long-suffering bridesmaids in boatloads of tulle and pastel ruffles; this will be an elegant production with simple, classic designs and muted shades.

Flowers that signify tradition are Capricorn's favorites—chrysanthemum, rose, and for a Christmastime wedding, poinsettia and holly. Visualize a dignified candlelight ceremony in the family church, the wedding party in dignified shades of tailored gray and bright red poinsettias everywhere, and a string quartet for accompaniment.

The Care and Feeding of Your Capricorn Marriage

THE PURPOSE OF A CAPRICORN MARRIAGE

The couple that marries when the Sun is in Capricorn feels an evolutionary urge to **build**. You'll always be at your best, as a couple, when you're drafting long-range goals and building structures that provide inspiration and sustenance for the largest possible number of people. Not content with raising just one small family, you are determined to contribute to the betterment of all of society—and working together, you have the opportunity to make a greater contribution than either of you could make separately.

WHAT THE CAPRICORN MARRIAGE NEEDS

In a word: **direction**. If you don't have a long-range plan to keep you moving forward, it's hard for you to feel really alive. You measure your happiness and progress in tangible results. This is not to imply that worldly achievement is more important to you than things of the heart, only to point out that you have a hard time knowing how you fit into the social fabric unless you are fulfilling some practical purpose.

So you need goals, objectively measured in outlines and lists, day planners and wall calendars. You need to have the sense of having built something together, and you need **recognition**, whether it's in the form of awards or simply a fiftieth wedding anniversary party where friends and family warmly celebrate your lives together. Most of all, you wish to leave a **legacy**—a body of work, and a spirit of charitable involvement and giving.

SOURCES OF FRICTION

Imagine you've come home at the end of a long day amongst the wild and uncivilized elements of the world. You're bone tired and a bit stressed out. It's dark and drizzling, cold and nasty. All you want to do is get home and sit in front of a roaring fire with a nice bowl of soup.

But as you pull into your driveway, you notice there isn't a single light burning inside the house. You dash through the rain, trip over a plant, fumble to find your key in the dark. You let yourself in and find no one else is home yet, and the cat begins hollering for some kibble. You feed the cat and rifle through the pantry for a can of soup, but as usual, no one has had time to go to the store—or to split firewood. You settle for a cold cheese sandwich in front of the wall heater ... but it's not quite the same.

A well-tended home shouldn't be a luxury, but when everyone is consumed with the work of the outside world, the domestic community can suffer. And a marriage and home that are neglected for too long can leave you both brittle and out of sorts. The primary challenge of the Capricorn marriage is to **balance outward achievement with inner contentment**—and the demands of the outside world with the needs of a home and family.

The Capricorn Marriage Style

THE FACE YOU SHOW THE WORLD

The face you show the world is as serious, professional, and trustworthy as Walter Cronkite in a pinstripe suit. Perhaps you both grew up as oldest children, looking after your youngest siblings or, perhaps, your immature and scattered parents. It's not coincidence that has drawn you toward your Capricorn marriage, but a deeply ingrained sense of responsibility and practical purpose!

WHAT YOU OWN

Mastering earthly existence is at the top of Capricorn's job description, and money and possessions are important earthly resources. As a team, you have a genius for transforming talents and raw materials into money; you are innovative and can see opportunities others don't.

You will probably do exceptionally well in building up whatever you consider to be a fortune—and that will likely set you apart from a lot of the other people in your lives. Your tendency may be to feel uncomfortable about this and go out of your way to downplay your good fortune. But better still is to share your genius with others, and to try to help them see opportunities for using their own skills and resources to their best advantage.

HOW YOU COMMUNICATE

Your idea of communication is not confined to talking—while you may well have plenty to say to each other, the lion's share of your communication takes place on an entirely different plane. In fact, your most profound communication takes place on an intuitive, spiritual level. If other parts of your marriage are floundering, however, you can easily slip into patterns of denial and avoid discussing problems until it's too late to solve them.

You may share a love of artistic expression such as music, poetry, art, or writing, and these are vital forms of communication between you. Those who see only your pragmatic, businesslike sides are surprised to find gentleness and a hint of fantasy in your words and ideas.

HOW YOU LIVE

Very likely you do a great deal of your work at home, and it's possible too that the work you do is connected in some way to domestic issues—construction, interior design, women's concerns. Your home is designed not for comfort, but for speed: you might as well put a revolving door at the entryway, because you both operate in perpetual overdrive.

Red is a particularly good color choice for your home; paint a wall crimson, or invest in a red slipcover for your sofa. Red's warmth and vibrancy are stimulating and cheerful and will help perk you up after long days fighting the battles of the outside world. If at all practical, choose a home with a working fireplace or wood stove; failing that, fill your home with candles and lanterns. Because they get the most use, the coziest rooms of your house will likely be your home offices. And your kitchen will be outfitted with a great cooktop and premium-quality knives—all of which rarely get used!

YOUR CHILDREN AND CREATIVE SPIRIT

For many Capricorn marriages, children are invited into the family simply out of traditional expectation, to perpetuate the family line, and for practical reasons, such as to help farm the land or run the family restaurant. It's not that you don't love your children; in fact, they probably give you great pleasure. You must resist the inclination to spoil them, and to protect them from facing the overwhelming difficulties you overcame in your own backgrounds. Remember, though, that these struggles allowed you to test your mettle and overcome adversity, which gave you confidence. The worst potential combination of Capricorn-style parenting is a combination of overprotection and ambition—pushing your children into roles that your parenting has not given them the confidence to perform well.

You enjoy your pleasures and recreation, and non-work hours—though few—are full of music, relaxed dinner parties, and leisurely games of golf, tennis, or cards. Creative expression, and friends who are merry and playful, provide pure pleasure and a welcome diversion from your worldly ambitions.

YOUR WORK, HEALTH, AND DAILY ROUTINE

The Capricorn marriage is often surprisingly traditional, with the male partner pursuing a career and the female partner monitoring home base. But whether or not you both pursue high-powered jobs for money, you are both sure to be incredibly busy. Your phone rings off the hook, people come and go at all hours, you travel, you write, and you're hardly ever at rest.

All this commotion, if not balanced by plenty of outdoor exercise and the occasional moratorium on communication, can fry your delicate nervous systems to a crisp. You are especially vulnerable to nervous stomachs and skin rashes, and when your bodies start sending you these unpleasant signals, it is time to take a break. A simple fifteen-minute bike ride in the middle of the day—not an indoor bike, either; you need fresh air and sunshine—will help give you a periodic boost of energy as well as keep you healthy.

YOUR FRIENDS AND FOES

Those you bring close into your fold are gentle, home-loving types. You spend long, happy hours at their big dining tables, eating delicious home-cooked food and admiring their children's artwork. They, in turn, rely on your sage advice and your practical, real-world acumen to help them cope with an overwhelming world.

The people who are most troublesome for your marriage are needy, clinging, and emotionally demanding. They sulk when you don't return their phone calls quickly enough, accuse you of looking down on them because they aren't as successful as you are, and feel that feeding you the occasional pot roast gives them the right to tell you everything that's wrong with your life. I need hardly advise practical folks like you to run from these so-called "friends" as fast and as far as you can!

WHAT YOU SHARE

You may behave a little formally with one another in public, but the intimate side of your marriage is surprisingly passionate. You enjoy each other, physically, mentally, and spiritually. This warm intimacy extends to sharing your combined resources; you are supportive of one another's goals and, together, are generous and warm-hearted when those you love are in need.

Romantic gestures, and the nurturing of a grand romantic narrative about your relationship, are important for keeping your marriage affectionate and lively. My uncle, a notorious curmudgeon, nevertheless kept a Christmas Eve ritual of shopping for his wife's anniversary present. He nearly always gave her some expensive but practical item she'd been longing for, but I always thought the really romantic gesture was his willingness to fight the crowds at the shopping mall on Christmas Eve, just to remember his wife on their wedding anniversary.

WHAT YOU BELIEVE

If you belong to a church, it's probably because everyone in your family has always belonged to it. Left to your own devices, you probably pursue more earthy spiritual observances, such as meditating on a mountaintop or while washing the kitchen floor.

Your beliefs are a fundamental component of your day-to-day lives together, but you feel strongly that treating people kindly in the here-and-now is much more meaningful than relying solely on rewards in the hereafter. You are critical thinkers, and any religion must satisfy your intellectual scrutiny or encourage deep and humble commitment to good and practical works.

YOUR CONTRIBUTION TO THE WORLD

Your careers are the glue that holds your marriage together. Here you are a smoothly functioning dynamic duo, comfortable in the public eye and unreservedly supportive of one another's goals. Usually one of you is the more "public" face of the relationship, but you both know that one partner's success is shared equally by the two of you.

The perfect example of this phenomenon is the Capricorn marriage of George H. W. and Barbara Bush. It's a union that has stood the test of time and had an important influence on two American presidencies. By all accounts, Barbara Bush, while wearing the public face of the "woman behind the man," is the true spine behind the ascendancy of the Bush dynasty.

YOUR PLACE IN SOCIETY

You are at ease among social groups comprising intense, passionate people of great conviction. Their careers often bring them in contact on a regular basis with the grittier sides of life—CIA operatives, police, detectives, psychologists, surgeons. As a couple, you dislike idle chitchat, and your idea of a great party features strenuous arguments that devolve quickly into lusty shouting around the dinner table.

Your entire view of the future is based on the fact that mortality is ever-present in the forefront of the Capricorn consciousness. It's likely that early trauma, such as the illness or death of someone close to you, has imprinted you with a keen appreciation for the transitory nature of life. Consequently, you have faith in your ability to survive. You live your lives as though there were no tomorrow, while at the same time you appreciate every moment you have.

YOUR PRIVATE SANCTUARY

To the world where you spend so much of your time and energy, you appear wise but perhaps a bit serious, and it's common for friends and family to urge you to slow down and enjoy life a bit more. But when no one else is around, you're actually funny, lively, optimistic, and philosophically engaged. You're readers and thinkers. You fantasize about being the King and Queen of everything. You go to the circus, speak in foreign languages, and dream big dreams you would be embarrassed to share in public, for fear (out of very normal Capricorn caution) that they will never come true. For similar reasons, joy, eagerness, and optimism are emotions you keep strictly under wraps.

There is also a religious side to your relationship that doesn't tend to express itself in allegiance to a denomination or to churchgoing, but which borrows from many faiths and includes a love of ritual and ceremony. Your work in the world is deeply influenced by your respect for religious beliefs and cultural differences, whether or not you belong to a church or espouse religious dogma in public.

The Aquarius Marriage
(JANUARY 21–FEBRUARY 18)

Famous Sun-in-Aquarius Marriages

Camille and Bill Cosby (January 25)
Danny DeVito and Rhea Perlman (January 28)
Paul Newman and Joanne Woodward (January 29)
Francis Ford and Eleanor Coppola (February 2)

❧

*A*quarius is often uncharitably depicted as a sign that loves mankind collectively, but not necessarily individually; is a friend to all, but to no one in particular; is happier in a group than one-on-one; and refuses to be reined in and insists on doing things in his or her own way.

What happens when a marriage begins under the influence of this detached, independent sign? If you assume it will be short-lived and tempestuous, you'll be surprised to find that Aquarius marriages seem to have a very good track record for longevity.

Show-business marriages are notoriously frequent and brief. Yet some of the entertainment world's most famous long-lasting marriages began with the Sun in Aquarius: Paul Newman and Joanne Woodward; Danny DeVito and Rhea Perlman; Camille and Bill Cosby; Francis Ford and Eleanor Coppola. All these marriages share something else in common: two partners with strong personalities and well-defined lives of their own, which they share out of choice rather than dependency.

This autonomous approach doesn't work for every couple. You need a lot of confidence in yourselves and trust in one another to offer each other quite so much latitude. For every Newman and Woodward that successfully walks the tightrope of autonomy and intimacy for half a century, there are surely a hundred couples who try this experiment and fail. The danger of sharing separate lives is that you may grow too far apart, and that one of you will be drawn into a relationship with someone whose interests lie closer to your own.

Both the potential benefits and drawbacks of the Aquarius marriage are, to some extent, the same ones faced by every single couple that decides to join their lives together. The benefits: a partnership of true equals and best friends who give each other freedom and space to do what they need to do. The drawbacks: a certain chilly distance, and the danger of waking up one morning wondering why in the world you're married to each other at all.

The Aquarius Season

The Sun is in Aquarius from late January through the first few weeks of February—in the Northern Hemisphere, the dead of winter, when the Sun is low in the sky and days are short. In astrology, likewise, Aquarius is considered one of the weakest signs for the Sun. This is not to say Aquarius people or marriages are weak—it only means that the principle of the Sun, of ego and the sovereignty of the individual, tends to be less well developed than in other signs. I happen to think this is a good thing for marriage, since a successful marriage is greatly helped by an attitude that emphasizes "us" instead of "me."

Aquarius is ruled by the planet Uranus, the mythical god of the sky. Before the discovery of Uranus, however, Saturn was assigned rulership of Aquarius in addition to his full-time job as ruler of Capricorn. Saturn is also considered very strong in Libra, the sign that rules marriage. So we know that the principles of maturity and responsibility symbolized by Saturn are beneficial to a successful marriage. Certainly Aquarius tends to be much more stable and reliable, even more conservative, than freedom-loving Uranus's rulership alone would suggest. Perhaps the longevity of so many Aquarius marriages is an expression of Saturn's sober influence.

The major holiday celebrated during the Aquarius season is St. Valentine's Day, which is celebrated with sentimental expressions of romantic affection, in particular flowers, candy, and greeting cards. On the face of it, all this romance seems strangely at odds with the astrological folklore associated with Aquarius. Ostensibly honoring one of at least three different Catholic saints named Valentine—none of whom has a particularly romantic history—modern St. Valentine's Day is probably a Christianization of Lupercalia, a pagan fertility festival that fell on the ides of February (February 15). This festival marked the beginning of ancient Roman spring by honoring Faunus, the Roman god of agriculture, fertility, and forests.

Astrological Aquarius, symbolized by the water bearer, is a sign of strong intellect and fixity of purpose—but also rebellion, accidents, and sudden change. It's as though the tension between mythical Uranus and his son, Saturn (who overthrew his father and seized power in a bloody coup) is channeled into one sign, producing explosive tension that is suddenly and periodically released. The marriage that begins when the Sun is in this fascinating sign likewise inherits the tension between Saturn's earthy stability, and Uranus's freedom-loving airiness.

How It Begins: The Aquarius Wedding

Astrologically, Aquarius is the sign that symbolizes shocking and unconventional style—but you needn't exchange vows while parachuting from a plane in order to have an unusual ceremony! The key is "unconventional," which is a relative concept. For instance, you might be the first among your siblings or peers to marry, or you may elope and present your marriage as a *fait accompli*. If the rest of your families have married in quiet, quirky ceremonies, yours is likely to be large and conventional. "Different" doesn't always mean "weird"!

Aquarius is a sociable, fraternal sign, so friends are likely to figure as prominently in your wedding as they will throughout your marriage. The wishes of your social circle are, in fact, more likely than those of your families to be taken into consideration when you choose a date or venue for your ceremony. However close you may be to your families individually, marrying during the Aquarius season suggests you have come together—at least in part—to declare your independence and begin new traditions that may directly contradict those you grew up with.

So wear what you like and throw convention to the wind. Dress your wedding party in the favorite colors of Aquarius—some combination of blue, silver, and just the right shade of purple. For flowers, choose tulips, symbolizing friendship; lots of greenery, especially ivy (ruled by Saturn) or a bit of holly; and unusually shaped flowers like daffodils, bird of paradise, or orchids.

The Care and Feeding of Your Aquarius Marriage

THE PURPOSE OF AN AQUARIUS MARRIAGE

The marriage that begins during the Aquarius season is destined to create progress. By serving as a nucleus for groups of people with a common purpose, and through your willingness to challenge the status quo and think in new ways, the Aquarius couple can help create real change in their communities. You will form a socially conscious team, attending city council meetings, volunteering to be poll workers, or even running for elected office yourselves. You have a strong sense that your destiny together lies in leaving the world better than you found it, and you're willing to roll up your sleeves and make that happen.

WHAT THE AQUARIUS MARRIAGE NEEDS

Above all, your Aquarius marriage needs to **share a sense of destiny**, the conviction that you are rowing the same boat toward a common goal—or at least complementary ones. Of all marriage signs, yours is the one that has the strongest sense of leaving a legacy for future generations. Unlike the Capricorn marriage, however, which creates dynasties within accepted social structures, the Aquarius marriage wants to leave legacies of social progress that address the limitations of those social structures.

Okay, so not everyone plays well with others. Aries, Leo, and Scorpio types, in particular, really dislike group projects. If you are born under one of these signs, you'll periodically tire of the constant group social engagements and long for a bit of quiet time, or even an intimate date with just your spouse.

Also, not all of us find it romantic or desirable to be best chums with our mates. It's true that the modern Western ideal of marriage includes respect and warm affection between marriage partners, such as one might feel for a good friend; but there is also the lingering belief that if your marriage partner is no more than a good friend, then you may as well have married any one of your pals. Most of us need to feel special, and that we arouse some carnal and romantic response in the hearts of our spouses, and this is a feeling that can sometimes elude you in an Aquarius marriage environment.

The Aquarius Marriage Style

THE FACE YOU SHOW THE WORLD

The Aquarius marriage is built on individuality and friendliness, and you consider the friendship you share to be much more important than the romantic dimension of your relationship. Associates may eventually comment that they doubt the existence of your spouse, since the two of you may seldom be seen together, busy as you are pursuing individual goals. When you are together in front of the world, you could easily be confused for good friends—which isn't so bad, when you consider how many ill-suited couples could be confused for mortal enemies.

WHAT YOU OWN

The Aquarius marriage tends to choose one of two distinct financial paths. One leads to financial disorganization and denial of fiscal realities; the other, to philanthropy and to a very high-minded, even spiritual relationship with money.

The story of "Newman's Own" is an example of the latter. When Paul Newman was coaxed into marketing his homemade salad dressing recipe to the public, he agreed on the condition that all proceeds from sales of the dressing be donated to charity (total contributions to date: more than $200 million). Meanwhile, Newman's wife, actress Joanne Woodward, raised the money to refurbish the historically important local community theater house in their hometown of Westport, Connecticut. It's important to keep in mind that having money doesn't make you any less spiritual, and that by treating your money conscientiously you may eventually find yourselves in a position to use it for noble purposes.

HOW YOU COMMUNICATE

You enjoy a good argument. To you, a spirited exchange of views clears the air, energizes your relationship, and is even kind of sexy. A subtle (or sometimes not so subtle) competition exists between you as to who can tell the wittiest joke or have the last word in an argument.

In extreme cases, among unbalanced people in an unhealthy relationship, this kind of communication has the potential to turn violent. O. J. Simpson and Nicole Brown were married with the Sun in Aquarius, and Simpson was arrested on a domestic violence charge to which he pleaded no contest. When Nicole and a male friend were found brutally murdered, Simpson was arrested on suspicion of the crimes (a jury later found him not guilty).

Of course, things will never become so unpleasant in the average Aquarius marriage. Still, in order to maintain your sense of mutual respect and friendship, it's a good idea to monitor your communication for signs that your spirited debates are becoming nasty or overheated.

HOW YOU LIVE

Your home is, above all, *comfortable*—with big, overstuffed pieces of furniture, nice china and silver, and luxurious bed linens and bath towels. Generally, the style will be fairly conservative; you crave comfort and appreciate quality, but dislike anything that's flashy or ostentatious. Your home is nearly always very clean and well-organized, and your idea of a good time is spending an afternoon at the Container Store.

You choose your home based on location—proximity to family members or work—and generally speaking, your real estate investments prove prudent. That is more or less academic, however, since once you've moved in you'll usually stay put for a good long time. Aquarius is a restless sign, but at the end of a long day acting as agents of societal change, you like to come home to something comfortable and familiar.

YOUR CHILDREN AND CREATIVE SPIRIT

You enjoy children and pets and your house is usually filled with both; if you have children at all, you will seldom have only one, and yours attract throngs of friends to your household. You find the noise, energy, and curiosity of children invigorating, and their chaos is music to your ears.

You also enjoy a variety of recreational and creative passions that keep you engaged. You embrace any hobbies, games, sports, or creative projects that allow you to visit regularly with neighbors and friends, meet new people, and pass the time in lively conversation.

YOUR WORK, HEALTH, AND DAILY ROUTINE

You like the security of regular routines and schedules, but you also require a little leeway to indulge your moods and whims. You may wake up and decide to eat dinner for breakfast and breakfast for lunch and popcorn for dinner; to go to the office two hours late and work late into the night. When you're forced into a rigid daily routine, your moods turn cranky and your health suffers.

Your prefer to deal with the world on an intellectual level, and unexpressed emotional upsets can also take their toll on your well-being. In the film *Broadcast News*, Holly Hunter plays a driven journalist who sets aside a few minutes every day to indulge in a good cry—whether or not she's feeling upset! While I don't necessarily recommend her methodology, it makes the point that venting your emotions regularly is very good for you.

YOUR FRIENDS AND FOES

Despite your friendliness and popularity, you're secretly a little bit afraid of not fitting in. And so you are drawn, as a couple, to people who appear very confident and outgoing, with a radiant sense of fun and enjoyment. They're performers, and you are good at providing an audience; it works out well for everyone. Most of these people are not only fine dinner party guests, they're extremely loyal, warm-hearted friends who would do absolutely anything for you.

But every personality has a shadow side. Sometimes the very confidence and joie de vivre that characterizes your closest friends can veer into an egocentric, even childish need to be at the center of every gathering. Know that when your friends begin to act like this, they're feeling just as insecure as you sometimes feel about not fitting in. Usually, people closest to us can mirror our shadow sides as well as our positive traits. Perhaps what these friends are demonstrating for you is that sometimes, the best way to feel good about ourselves is to help others feel good about themselves.

WHAT YOU SHARE

You share a strong, earthy physical attraction that endures well past the honeymoon, perhaps because it is accompanied by a passionate meeting of the minds. Resist the urge to criticize one another, though; it's a mood killer, in or out of the bedroom.

You're comfortable and adept managers of your shared resources, and are frugal, conscientious stewards of your capital. Your checkbook is balanced, your coupons are clipped, and you are among the few people who actually read the annual reports you receive from the companies in your portfolio. If anything, you may be a little *too* attentive to your investments, to the point of needless worry. Set aside a regular time each week or month to review your accounts, and then let the dollars take care of themselves.

WHAT YOU BELIEVE

You dream big dreams, the two of you; it's as though when you married each other the world grew ten sizes larger overnight. The possibilities for what you might achieve seem limitless, because you have each other for inspiration and support. It's possible the two of you come from quite different backgrounds; it's your differences, rather than your similarities, which really drew you to one another.

You will particularly love to travel together, and if you're unable to travel far, you will substitute with adventures in your own community—trying new restaurants, energetically pursuing outdoor activities, and exploring parts of town that are unfamiliar to you. Religions, especially religions different from the ones you grew up with, are a source of endless fascination to you, and a shared belief system is a cornerstone of your relationship.

YOUR CONTRIBUTION TO THE WORLD

Without knowing you very well at all, people tend to find you a little intimidating. They sense that you are private about your personal lives, and that actually makes you especially intriguing!

But you also seem trustworthy. Aquarius is able to find the common link between people, and as a couple you instinctively find common ground with everyone you meet. Others identify with you, no matter how different you actually are from one another. There's a peculiar tension between your surface friendliness and the guardedness that others encounter as they get to know you better.

You are extremely focused, even obsessed, about your careers, and you are particularly well suited to occupations that involve research, diagnostics, or psychology; clandestine careers such as detective work; or work that helps people transform their lives. You're private about your own affairs, but others are all too eager to share their secrets with you!

YOUR PLACE IN SOCIETY

Your natural social group is educated, well-traveled, and cultured—but not above a night of feasting and ribald jokes! You often find kindred souls through school or through political or religious affiliations.

Your ideal friends are people you can *do* things with—sports, hiking, games. These are activities that, along with travel, will keep you young well into your senior years.

You encourage a sense of far-reaching optimism in one another, and are apt to be rather cheerful, upbeat senior citizens. Your greatest insurance against crankiness and bitterness in old age is constant exposure to different cultures and beliefs. Maintaining a sense of wonder and excitement is your fountain of youth.

YOUR PRIVATE SANCTUARY

You don't like to be alone. You associate solitude with loneliness and want, and behind your friendliness is a horror of growing old alone. If you find a way to befriend solitude, though, you will find a rich fount of fortitude and vast reserves of strength.

In fact, you have a tremendous reverence for the elderly, and probably do more for your aging relatives and other elderly people than anyone ever finds out about. Yours is a pragmatic approach, though, and you are more apt to organize fundraising events than to sit and read with the elderly, on the basis that you can help more people that way.

The Pisces Marriage
(FEBRUARY 19–MARCH 20)

Famous Sun-in-Pisces Marriages

Kurt Cobain and Courtney Love (February 24)
Johnny Cash and June Carter Cash (March 1)
Paul McCartney and Linda Eastman (March 12)
Franklin D. and Eleanor Roosevelt (March 17)

❧

*I*t's a prototypically Piscean fairy tale: good-hearted woman meets hard-living man and saves him from his boozin', drug-abusin', womanizin' ways. The redeeming power of love is a timeless romantic theme, second in popularity only to the ideal of a romantic love that lasts a lifetime. Occasionally, the two dovetail, as in the true-life love story of country music legends Johnny Cash and his wife, June Carter Cash.

Cash was already both a country music star and a floundering alcoholic and drug addict when he met June Carter, of the legendary bluegrass family. Both were married to other partners, so their relationship began as a warm friendship but gradually grew more passionate. As Cash descended further into his addiction, eventually endangering his career, Carter tried to help her friend—and gradually realized she had fallen in love with him. But even after Johnny got straight, June needed convincing that this man was a safe bet. By the time he proposed to her—on stage during a concert—she was ready to accept. They were married on March 1, 1968, and remained married until Carter Cash's death in 2003. Johnny died four months later.

By marrying two of show business's most eligible bachelors, Paul McCartney and Warren Beatty, Linda Eastman and Annette Benning undertook "reform" of a different sort. There was little in the previous relationships of these notorious ladies' men to suggest they would ever settle down and be happy in marriage. Yet the McCartneys' marriage (which began on March 12, 1969) was legendarily close; the two famously spent only a few nights apart over the course of their twenty-nine-year marriage. Beatty and Benning married in 1992, and as of 2007 they've been married fifteen years and are raising four children together.

It's notable that the Pisces marriage often features a theme of redemption or healing, with one partner serving as helpmate to the other. Consider the Pisces marriage of President Franklin D. and Eleanor Roosevelt. After Franklin contracted crippling polio, Eleanor became his "legs"—not to mention his eyes and ears—visiting far-flung parts of the country and reporting back to her husband about what the people of the nation were feeling and experiencing.

Sometimes, the fairy tale goes awry and the Pisces marriage slides into Neptune's shadow side of drugs, confinement, or self-destruction. Rockers Kurt Cobain and Courtney Love, married February 24, 1992, had by all accounts a tempestuous marriage complicated by drug use and Cobain's emotional problems. Neptune, Pisces' ruling planet, symbolizes fluid boundaries—between ourselves and others, and between reality and illusion—and Neptune's waters can contain treacherous rocks for those who struggle to maintain a grip on reality. Sadly, Cobain ended his life in 1994.

Unconditional love is a hallmark of the Pisces marriage. But committing yourself to a lifetime of selfless devotion to another person is a gamble that doesn't always pay off. The Pisces marriage offers the greatest chance for happiness when both partners are reasonably stable, responsible, and devoted to one another's well-being.

The Pisces Season

The Sun is in Pisces from late February through the first few weeks of March, when the weather in the Northern Hemisphere is cool, windy, and rainy. It's not a terribly popular time of year to marry, and it's not necessarily a practical choice of season for a lavish, modern wedding. The Pisces season lends itself more naturally to a quieter celebration—

an informal ceremony before the justice of the peace, an intimate gathering at home, or a vacation wedding in a tropical climate, attended by only a few close friends.

Pisces is ruled by the planets Jupiter and Neptune, named for the king of the gods and the god of the sea, respectively. Astrologically, Pisces "goes with the flow," able to grasp the mood of every situation and to empathize with almost anyone. It is a gentle and compassionate sign, but it is possessed, too, of Jupiter's enormous strength, luck, and charisma. A marriage that begins during Pisces' season can be astonishingly resilient, blessed by Jupiter's fortune and Neptune's gift for accepting life—and other people—as they are. The key to happiness for the Pisces marriage is to be able to enter the mystery of understanding another person, all the while keeping a firm grip on who you are.

How It Begins: The Pisces Wedding

Dreamy, sensitive, and spiritually aware: Pisces is a hopeless romantic, but does not care for strict schedules or complex planning. A complicated wedding with challenging logistics is not really Pisces' style. A ceremony that's simple, heartfelt, and informal, even impromptu, is the appropriate beginning to a Pisces marriage.

Honor Neptune if you can by marrying near water—on a beach, next to a river or swimming pool, or even at an aquarium. Gauzy, transparent fabrics, fairy lights, flickering candles, and colors of the ocean suit Pisces' freeform style. Pisces happily embraces all cultures, so consider including elements from other traditions—folk music, a unity candle, a ketubah, or poetry.

Drape your ceremony in the colors of the ocean—sea greens, gray blues, and iridescent shades are perfect for the Pisces wedding, especially when matched with violet. Violets, in fact, are flowers closely associated with Pisces. The violet, which has small purple or white flowers, flourishes in the cool months of early spring. In Greek myth, violets were sacred to the god Aries and to Io, one of Zeus's lovers. Christian symbolism associated the violet with humility, or humble modesty, and several legends describe violets appearing on the graves of virgins and saints. A humble flower for the most modest and spiritual of signs.

Another flower that is appropriate for Pisces is the poppy. The Greeks associated poppies with both Hypnos, god of sleep, and Morpheus, god of dreams. Morphine, a drug made from opium, gets its name from Morpheus. Jonquils are plentiful and traditionally associated with March, but be careful: they're poisonous and can be fatal if eaten.

The Care and Feeding of Your Pisces Marriage

THE PURPOSE OF A PISCES MARRIAGE

The Pisces union exists to provide unconditional love and support, for both partners as well as their families, friends, and extended social network. At its best, the Pisces household is a refuge where those who are troubled or in need can make their way and receive solace and empathy. Imagine the Pisces marriage as a lighthouse, helping weary travelers make their way safely to shore without crashing on the rocks.

WHAT THE PISCES MARRIAGE NEEDS

Above all, the Pisces marriage needs **inspiration**. You need plenty of joy, fun, and hope in your daily lives; excessive negativity, nay-saying, and criticism will actually damage your marriage.

The healthy Pisces marriage is full of music, art, and travel, and is devoted to spiritual practice. You are confident enough to let yourselves appear "flaky" and "New-Agey" by pursuing offbeat interests; you're much less interested in proving yourselves than in enjoying life and exploring new ideas and cultures.

SOURCES OF FRICTION

Of course, not every kind of personality finds it easy to flourish in the Pisces marriage. A driven, ambitious, or strongly egocentric character might find the waters of the Pisces marriage inhospitable, as might those with a love of precision, detail, and schedules. If you are a task-driven person in a Pisces marriage, make an effort to relax into the fluid Pisces style. Because Pisces doesn't yield to the tyranny of schedules and clocks, you may find you are actually able to accomplish much more than you ever have before, because you're not preoccupied with running out of time!

The Pisces Marriage Style

THE FACE YOU SHOW THE WORLD

At first, people may not notice you at all: Pisces has the ability to disappear when it wants to. And of course, not every Pisces marriage has the high profile of the Cashes or McCartneys. But when people are first getting to know you, it will generally be through a spiritual/social, health-related, or artistic dimension of your lives together. You initially become intertwined in their minds so that you no longer appear to be two individuals, but rather a single entity. They will think you are kind, think you are pleasant, and the less scrupulous of them will think they can run roughshod over you.

They're in for a surprise.

WHAT YOU OWN

While unstructured and laissez-faire in many areas of your lives together, you're surprisingly directed and energetic in the area of earning money—and once you have it, you tend to be a bit impulsive about the way you spend it. Words like "burn" tend to pepper your money-related conversations: "money to burn," "burning through our capital," "burning a hole in our pockets." You will likely be early adopters of new gadgets, purchased at top-of-the-market prices.

If one or the other of you was born under a more prudent sign such as Cancer or Virgo, you may have a better chance of holding on to some of your money. Otherwise, your best chance for a financially secure future lies in educating yourselves about investments. Make investing a game by setting financial goals for regular intervals and challenging yourselves to meet them. A competitive spirit will motivate you in a positive direction and make you less apt to "burn through" your assets.

HOW YOU COMMUNICATE

From time to time, you may forget to talk to each other. It's not that you have nothing to say, but rather that you rely on nonverbal forms of communication more than some couples do. Perhaps you communicate through music, like Pisces marriage couples Paul and Linda McCartney, Johnny and June Carter Cash, and Kurt Cobain and Courtney Love. Touch is another effective and healing form of communication between the two of you.

You are susceptible to stubborn, circular arguments, though, so if you occasionally reach a communication impasse, it might help to throw yourselves into a shared project that yields tangible results. Gardening, cooking, or home renovation projects create a relaxed but productive atmosphere that gives you plenty of time to gather and share your thoughts.

HOW YOU LIVE

You enjoy variety in your home, and prefer a house with many rooms, each for a distinct purpose. You are likely to have more than one home (such as a primary residence and a vacation home) or to live in a duplex, apartment building, or condominium with more than one unit. Something about this arrangement satisfies your need for diversity and options in your living situation.

Your home is a hive of activity, with a revolving door of guests, friends, children, and neighbors coming and going, calling on the phone, staying for a week, borrowing your car. You love words and encourage reading; books and magazines clutter every available surface that isn't taken up with computers, and you may even stencil inspiring quotations on your walls.

YOUR CHILDREN AND CREATIVE SPIRIT

You adore children and are probably less likely to remain childless than most couples. You are parents to the world, including nieces and nephews and friends of your own children, and you will be ideal grandparents. You may even adopt children, become foster parents, or act as mentors to young people. The idea of children being neglected, hungry, or homeless fills you with intense sadness.

You are also an extremely creative couple, capable of producing art, music, or writing that is profoundly moving. Many couples struggle to balance parenting with creative endeavors, but the two of you provide so much nurturing for each other's projects, and those of your children, that there is more than enough energy and focus to go around.

YOUR WORK, HEALTH, AND DAILY ROUTINE

You are not slaves to schedules, but interestingly enough you do enjoy fixed routines and like to anchor your days with certain predictable rituals. Be sure you include healthy meals and regular sleep among those rituals. And be conscious of your habits; unhealthy patterns, should they sneak into your routine, will be just as enduring as healthy ones.

You are drawn to work in relatively glamorous fields such as entertainment, metaphysics, the arts, writing, fashion, or performance. As a couple, you have a gift for motivating and inspiring others. The difficulty lies in balancing your extreme sensitivity with the extroverted and dynamic work environments to which you are drawn.

YOUR FRIENDS AND FOES

People close to you often mistake your gentleness for timidity or lack of direction and try to jump in and organize your lives for you. You can benefit from the practical, linear, organized approach to life that comes naturally to many of your friends, just as they would do well to learn from your accepting "live and let live" philosophy. Try not to take criticism too personally; the people close to you generally mean well, and worry that you will be taken advantage of by a cruel world because you are so trusting.

But of course, not everyone has your best interests at heart. "Friends" who are overly critical, chronically pessimistic, or excessively interfering will contribute little to your happiness—and will rarely let you contribute to theirs.

WHAT YOU SHARE

The intimate side of your relationship thrives on good taste, impeccable hygiene, and a healthy dose of good, old-fashioned romance. Traditional wooing rituals such as candlelit dinners, flowers, and sentimental gifts fuel the passionate side of your relationship.

These traditional courtship roles may extend to your handling of shared finances, with one partner taking control of the checkbook and the other drawing an allowance. In order to maintain balance and harmony in your relationship, however, a healthier approach is to take equal responsibility for making sure your accounts are balanced and your investments in order.

WHAT YOU BELIEVE

Deeply interested in profound questions of life and death, you are passionate travelers, religious seekers, and lovers of knowledge. You engage in passionate debates about culture, spirituality, and truth and are willing to delve into esoteric subjects that most people avoid. You have a special fascination for subjects related to spiritual sexuality, such as tantric yoga.

The cultures that fascinate you are always very exotic, with strong colors, tastes, and smells, and art that is provocative and often sexually explicit. They provide an exciting contrast to your everyday world of soft oceanic colors, gentle music, and delicate romance.

YOUR CONTRIBUTION TO THE WORLD

Teaching, publishing, speaking, education, and ministry are natural career paths for the Pisces marriage. Together and individually, you are drawn to careers that allow you to explore life's philosophical, religious, and cultural dimensions, and to share your understanding of these things.

You are ambitious, but not in the sense of acquiring a fortune or great wealth; rather, you have ambitious dreams, and encourage each other to think big and reach for the moon. You feel you are destined to make a great contribution to your chosen fields, and as long as your dreams are grounded in usefulness and preparation, there is no reason you can't.

YOUR PLACE IN SOCIETY

You're actually rather private people, and your social circle tends to be limited to members of your family and business associates. You would like to be involved in social organizations, but too often you find that you are placed in positions of authority and take on too much responsibility, so you generally prefer to do good works on an individual basis.

Perhaps because you generally adopt such a relaxed attitude toward life, your chances of remaining healthy and productive well into old age are greatly improved. You will, in fact, become more youthful with age, as the burdens of making a living fall away and you are able to relax and turn your attention to matters closer to your hearts—art, spiritual reflection, and dreams.

YOUR PRIVATE SANCTUARY

No matter how gentle and sweet you appear to the world, you are rebels and revolutionaries at heart. You may spend every night together under the same roof, but you are much more independent, autonomous, and individualistic than you may seem. Linda McCartney, for example, played keyboards and sang in her husband's band, but she also built a successful vegetarian cooking empire in the years she spent married to Paul.

The secret no one knows about you is that despite your ability to blend into any situation, you fear becoming so enmeshed in other people's concerns that you risk losing your own identities completely. So you have developed a secret weapon: the ability to suddenly detach and disappear, like ships lifting anchor in the darkness of night. You seldom use this weapon, and even when you do, you eventually make your way back to shore; but it gives you peace of mind to know that if you need to, you can make a clean, quick getaway.

Your Best Marriage Signs

*I*magine that your best friend has moved into a new house. By any objective standard, it's a beauty—large, modern, and roomy, with plenty of light, state-of-the-art fixtures, and lavish furnishings. Your friend loves her house. All your friends admire it.

Why, then, do you absolutely hate it?

From the moment you walk through the door until you finally leave, you feel fidgety and uncomfortable amidst the richly carpeted floors and granite countertops. It's beautiful, but it's simply *not your style*. You can't wait to get home to your worn, gently shabby Queen Anne Victorian across town, with its scarred hardwood floors and balky windows, its built-in nooks and antique plumbing.

Style is subjective, both in homes and in marriages. A marriage is very much like a house that you move into on your wedding day, and like a house it has a certain architectural style. You can decorate a house any way you like, but let's face it: a new slipcover for the sofa won't turn an arts-and-crafts bungalow into a mid-century modern.

The Sun's sign on your wedding day describes the architectural style of your union—much as your own Sun sign describes how you are built. Some marriage styles mesh easily with your own personality and feel comfortable to you right from the start; another might require years of refurbishing before it really feels like home. By understanding the relationship between your birth sign and your marriage sign, you will know which is the more likely scenario!

If You Were Born with the Sun in Aries

Born at the beginning of spring, your cosmic birth assignment is to cultivate assertiveness, courage, and a strong sense of self. Nature constantly seeks balance, and so you unconsciously seek partners who complement your own independent, headstrong nature, partners with good manners, social acumen, and a graceful knack for compromise. The Aries man seeks a partner he can place on a pedestal; the Aries woman, for all her independence, has a soft spot for a knight on a white horse, a man she can look up to. Both do best in a marriage that offers maximum independence and a spirited sense of give-and-take.

BEST MARRIAGE SIGNS FOR ARIES

- **Aries** (March 21–April 20). The needs of the Aries marriage match your own: self-sufficiency, entrepreneurialism, and courage in taking risks. On the minus side, there may be little opposition to temper the brasher, less sensitive tendencies of your birth sign.

- **Gemini** (May 22–June 21). Marriage while the Sun is in Gemini offers enough variety and movement to satisfy your preference for speed and action. You are less a person of words than deeds, however, which may occasionally be a problem within this most communicative of marriages.

- **Leo** (July 24–August 23). Marriage while the Sun is in Leo is a real love match for you. The Leo marriage features partners who are equally committed to creative pursuits and fun; you will bring the added bonus of directedness and leadership, which will keep your marriage from getting too "stuck."

- **Libra** (September 24–October 23). The Libra marriage offers one of your best environments for growth. The Libra marriage is "other-oriented," and to succeed, it requires both partners to think of the other person first. To say this does not come naturally to you is an understatement! View your Libra marriage as the ultimate challenge, however, and you will be motivated to give it your very best effort.

- **Sagittarius** (November 23–December 21). The Sagittarius marriage thrills by inviting you to use your drive and determination to succeed in ever-larger arenas. If you are, for instance, an Aries artist, your Sagittarius marriage will provide an environment that exposes you to a whole new world of inspiration and opportunities, and inspire you to reach for the moon.

- **Aquarius** (January 21–February 18). The Aquarius marriage has a social network of staggering breadth, with a variety of groups, friends, and like-minded contacts to inspire you. By emphasizing your natural independence, however, it may weaken the bonds of intimacy and fidelity that are so important to a marriage.

If You Were Born with the Sun in Taurus

Born in the lush indolence of mid-spring, your cosmic birth assignment is to cultivate security and a strong appreciation of life's joys and beauty. To keep you from becoming complacent, you unconsciously seek partners who complement your easy-going contentment with a spirit of intensity, drama, and psychological conflict. The Taurus man seeks a partner with mysterious sexual allure; the Taurus woman, for all her practicality, is drawn to men who seem complex and a little bit dangerous. Both sexes do best in a marriage that offers trust, security, and a healthy balance of contentment and intrigue.

BEST MARRIAGE SIGNS FOR TAURUS

- **Taurus** (April 21–May 21). The Taurus style of marriage is slow, languid, measured, and it perfectly reflects your individual style. There is little to challenge you, though, and the danger is that you will become too complacent and your life quite dull.

- **Cancer** (June 22–July 23). The Cancer marriage is oriented toward home, hearth, family, and security—a perfect mix for your own stability, contentment, and delight in life's simplest pleasures.

- **Virgo** (August 24–September 23). The Virgo marriage is practical, service-oriented, and analytical, which is compatible with your own pragmatic nature. However, this marriage will challenge you to think things through instead of just "doing what comes naturally."

- **Scorpio** (October 24–November 22). The Scorpio marriage is a self-improvement laboratory, intensely reflective and geared toward personal empowerment. It is a very challenging environment for someone like you, who isn't terribly introspective by nature; but it can provide a balance that keeps you from becoming too bound by habit and convention.

- **Capricorn** (December 22–January 20). The Capricorn marriage wants to build a dynasty, whether through business, politics, or personal power. You don't care much about those things, but you respect them—and you enjoy the creature comforts they can provide.

- **Pisces** (February 19–March 20). The Pisces marriage thrives in a gentle, dreamy environment of music, art, and spiritual interests, taking care of others and committing random acts of kindness. All that spiritual stuff may seem a little precious to you, but you certainly appreciate music and art, and you will enjoy providing the ballast for your rather ethereal marriage.

If You Were Born with the Sun in Gemini

Above all, your cosmic job description demands that you **stay curious**, never stop learning, and constantly communicate with others about your observations. To keep you from becoming too scattered, you unconsciously seek partners who complement your restless curiosity with a deep conviction about which ideas and experiences are worth holding on to and nurturing. The Gemini man seeks a partner who is religious or culturally exotic; the Gemini woman will always be a sucker for a man with a cute foreign accent. Both sexes do best in a marriage that offers good conversation, an exchange of ideas, and a healthy balance between conviction and questioning.

BEST MARRIAGE SIGNS FOR GEMINI

- **Aries** (March 21–April 20). The Aries marriage encourages pioneering into new and exciting situations, which feeds your need for variety. Being a pioneer, however, requires a conviction that you should move in a particular direction, at least for a while, and that might be difficult for you.

- **Gemini** (May 22–June 21). Marriage while the Sun is in Gemini completely validates your restlessness and inquisitive nature, encouraging you to remain somewhat detached from much of what goes on around you. There is little, however, to curb your tendency toward shallowness.

- **Leo** (July 24–August 23). Marriage while the Sun is in Leo provides a very good environment for you. It nurtures the ability to stay with some of your ideas long enough to create something fun and interesting from them. It also encourages opportunities to meet a great many people and to make fairly close friends of many of them.

- **Libra** (September 24–October 23). The Libra marriage is heaven on earth for your bright, interested, chatty personality. You and your partner create a marital atmosphere that is perfect for exchanging ideas.

- **Sagittarius** (November 23–December 21). The Sagittarius marriage emphasizes the search for meaning and truth, which provides a steadying balance to your quest for ideas and penchant for asking questions. This marriage will provide a growth opportunity for you.

- **Aquarius** (January 21–February 18). The Aquarius marriage has a social network that will delight the Gemini's soul, and emphasizes independence. The Aquarius marriage, however, focuses you toward long-term goals and social responsibility, which requires a conviction and fixity of purpose that presents challenges for you.

If You Were Born with the Sun in Cancer

Born at the height of summer, when all is slow and meditative, your cosmic imperative is to provide a womb for the nurturing of creative impulses. To prevent your perspective from becoming too narrowly focused on your own home and family, you instinctively seek partners who concentrate on more worldly concerns. The Cancer man seeks a partner with the ability the set aside emotional complications and tackle any task at hand; the Cancer woman, however emancipated, is drawn to men who seem like good providers (or like her father). Both sexes do best in a marriage that offers a good balance between family life and healthy career ambition.

BEST MARRIAGE SIGNS FOR CANCER

- **Taurus** (April 21–May 21). The Taurus style of marriage provides an earthy, stable, practical environment that is the perfect complement to your hair-trigger emotionalism. The steadiness of Taurus offers the security you crave.

- **Cancer** (June 22–July 23). The Cancer marriage is oriented toward home, hearth, family, and security. It's such a comfortable match for you that you may never leave the house!

- **Virgo** (August 24–September 23). The Virgo marriage is practical, service-oriented, and analytical, which is compatible with your own nurturing, caretaking personality. You will need to safeguard against taking on too many sad cases and overtaxing your energy and resources.

- **Scorpio** (October 24–November 22). The Scorpio marriage emphasizes trust, loyalty, and deep emotional commitment—absolutely perfect for Cancer, who craves constant reassurance of love and security.

- **Capricorn** (December 22–January 20). The Capricorn marriage will distract you from your single-minded concentration on your own family and immediate environment, and encourage your interest in society as a whole. This is among the healthiest marriage seasons for you, because it will support you to transcend your boundaries in a way that is often difficult for you—but is necessary.

- **Pisces** (February 19–March 20). The Pisces marriage provides a gentle environment of peace, rest, and compassionate outreach, and appeals to your gentle, quiet side. You tend to be very directed, so you can help bring much-needed focus to the marriage—and in turn, will learn to relax a little bit.

If You Were Born with the Sun in Leo

You are here to **entertain**, to **create**, and to **inspire others**. To keep yourself from becoming too self-absorbed, you unconsciously seek partners who are strange and quirky enough to divert your attention from your own vision. The Leo man seeks a partner who is independent, with more than enough friends and interests to keep herself busy; the Leo woman will always be drawn to brainy, mad-scientist types who seem to barely notice when she's in the room. Both sexes do best in a marriage that keeps them a bit off balance with a graceful combination of detachment and adoration.

BEST MARRIAGE SIGNS FOR LEO

- **Aries** (March 21–April 20). The Aries marriage is wildly passionate and exciting, and Leo will be right at home with its spirit of fairy-tale romance.

- **Gemini** (May 22–June 21). Marriage when the Sun is in Gemini promises a lifetime of variety, entertainment, and terrific conversation, which suits Leo just fine. What might prove grating over the long haul is Gemini's changeable, restless quality; Leo may be many things, but "flighty" is not among them.

- **Leo** (July 24–August 23). Marry when the Sun is in Leo, and you will be the biggest star in a wedding that will have a movie-star quality all its own. This marriage will do little, though, to temper your tendency toward self-centeredness.

- **Libra** (September 24–October 23). The Libra marriage is built on equality and mutual respect, which is perfect for Leo—as long as he or she marries a true equal, not just a "yes" man or woman.

- **Sagittarius** (November 23–December 21). The Sagittarius marriage encourages you to think big and live large, and this suits Leo down to the ground. There is an emphasis on individual freedom, though, that can irritate possessive Leo.

- **Aquarius** (January 21–February 18). The Aquarius marriage offers stability, excitement, and eccentricity—the perfect formula for keeping Leo intrigued and delighted. This marriage is a democracy, though, not a monarchy, and that can be an adjustment for regal Leos.

If You Were Born with the Sun in Virgo

Born at the very end of summer, your cosmic birth assignment is to cultivate precision and to bring a sense of order to life. To complement your vigilance for detail and reverence for structure, you unconsciously seek partners who resist barriers and embrace everyone and everything with unconditional regard. Virgo men and women alike seek partners who are sweet, compassionate, and artistic; often, until they realize what they're really looking for, they attract the lost, hazy, and irresponsible. Both sexes do best in a marriage that offers a comfortable balance of logic and belief, rationality and magic.

BEST MARRIAGE SIGNS FOR VIRGO

- **Taurus** (April 21–May 21). Marrying while the Sun is in Taurus provides an atmosphere that encourages your practical, earthy side, which is comfortable. It does little, though, to encourage you to nurture the more emotional, intuitive side of your nature.

- **Cancer** (June 22–July 23). The Sun-in-Cancer marriage emphasizes nurturing, family, and emotional attachments, which is a good fit for you. You enjoy helping people but are sometimes adrift in attending to their emotional needs, and this marriage will help you develop those skills.

- **Virgo** (August 24–September 23). The Sun-in-Virgo marriage is perfectly suited to your logical, pragmatic, problem-solving orientation. However, you will need to guard against becoming overly invested in your rational side and undernourishing your intuitive, spiritual side.

- **Scorpio** (October 24–November 22). Marrying when the Sun is in Scorpio provides an atmosphere of emotional intensity and depth that provides a powerful counterpoint to your practical earthiness. You may find the drama of this union a bit of a distraction from your everyday concerns and obligations—but to a reasonable extent, this is a good thing.

- **Capricorn** (December 22–January 20). The Sun-in-Capricorn marriage encourages worldly ambition and systematic pursuit of goals, which speaks perfectly to your strongest skills: organization and analysis. You may be inclined to work a little too hard within this marriage, though, and will need to rely upon your partner to remind you when you need to rest and recharge.

- **Pisces** (February 19–March 20). The Sun-in-Pisces marriage, with its easy-going, dreamlike, in-the-moment atmosphere, is the ultimate challenge for you—and as such, provides your best opportunity for a marriage that really helps you grow and achieve balance.

If You Were Born with the Sun in Libra

You were born to **collaborate with**, **harmonize with**, and **complement** everything and everyone in your environment. To keep you from becoming too accommodating, you unconsciously seek the challenge of partners who are strongly individualistic and confrontational. The Libra man needs a partner who is confident, determined, and assertive; the Libra woman is magnetized by strong, physical, uncomplicated partners. Both sexes do best in a marriage that balances rugged individualism with graceful accommodation, resulting in a true union of equals.

BEST MARRIAGE SIGNS FOR LIBRA

- **Aries** (March 21–April 20). The Aries marriage challenges all your assumptions about togetherness and compatibility, because it is an environment that encourages directness and assertiveness. You must fight to make this marriage work, and while that may fray your nerves, it will also make you stronger.

- **Gemini** (May 22–June 21). A marriage with the Sun in Gemini provides an environment of variety, wit, and networking that offers you endless opportunities to use your charm and satisfy your need for socializing.

- **Leo** (July 24–August 23). If the Sun is in Leo when you marry, expect a marriage that is romantic, fun, and passionate—if a little overwhelming for your delicate sensibilities.

- **Libra** (September 24–October 23). The Libra marriage prospers in an atmosphere of equality and mutual respect, which comes naturally for you. The danger is that there may be little of the friction required to keep you from becoming *too* accommodating.

- **Sagittarius** (November 23–December 21). The Sun-in-Sagittarius marriage encourages big dreams and unbridled enthusiasm, which is fine for helping you and your partner attract the fine things that, to you, make life worth living.

- **Aquarius** (January 21–February 18). Like your own birth sign, Aquarius favors relationships between equals, and this should be a convivial marital environment for you. The Aquarius marriage may, however, offer less time with your spouse than you would like.

If You Were Born with the Sun in Scorpio

Born in the middle of autumn's decay, your path in life lies in accepting the inevitable end of all things and celebrating the contrast between life and death. To balance your need to confront and acknowledge endings, you unconsciously seek happy, uncomplicated partners who embrace the simplest and heartiest of life's pleasures. Scorpio men and women seek contented partners who enjoy nature, food and drink, and the arts. Both sexes do best in a marriage that offers a stimulating balance of passion and contentment, and of the natural and the supernatural.

BEST MARRIAGE SIGNS FOR SCORPIO

- **Taurus** (April 21–May 21). Marrying while the Sun is in Taurus provides an atmosphere that cultivates calm, patience, and simple happiness. It may sometimes, however, feel a bit lacking in the passion and drama that is an essential part of your nature.

- **Cancer** (June 22–July 23). The Sun-in-Cancer marriage promotes a strong sense of roots and family belonging, which is sweet and nurturing for a soul who is keenly aware of life's threatening side. You are strongly protective of those you love, and this marriage will provide many opportunities to explore that side of your personality.

- **Virgo** (August 24–September 23). The Sun-in-Virgo marriage has a focus toward analysis of problems and practical assistance. There is a comforting pragmatism to this marriage sign that provides a healthy balance to your probing, emotionally insightful nature.

- **Scorpio** (October 24–November 22). Marrying when the Sun is in Scorpio provides an atmosphere of emotional intensity and depth that harmonizes perfectly with your intrinsic nature. If you are in command of your emotions, this marriage sign will provide a powerful environment for transformative and healing work.

- **Capricorn** (December 22–January 20). Marriage with the Sun in Capricorn encourages practical achievement and social consciousness. It offers a useful framework for your own ambitious and powerfully transformative nature.

- **Pisces** (February 19–March 20). The Sun-in-Pisces marriage is a spiritual haven that demands a certain surrender of personal ego and desire; this will present a profound challenge to you, but one that is potentially deeply satisfying to the spiritual side of your personality.

If You Were Born with the Sun in Sagittarius

Your life's path compels you to **explore new ideas**, from which you formulate visions and generate scholarship. To prevent you from becoming too enamored of your own opinions, you unconsciously seek partners who question your beliefs. The Sagittarius man seeks a partner who is curious, articulate, and able to juggle the minutiae of daily life; the Sagittarius woman is fascinated by witty, charming, unpredictable partners. Both sexes do best in a marriage that cultivates strong convictions informed by a steady flow of fresh information and inquiry.

BEST MARRIAGE SIGNS FOR SAGITTARIUS

- **Aries** (March 21–April 20). The Aries marriage encourages directness and ambition, two qualities Sagittarius very much admires. However, it is a marriage atmosphere more congenial to quick thinking and fast action rather than the deep, philosophical explorations of which you are fond.

- **Gemini** (May 22–June 21). Marriage when the Sun is in Gemini is filled with variety, curiosity, and entertaining conversation. By ensuring a steady stream of new people and experiences in your life, your marriage will keep you from becoming too entrenched in one way of thinking.

- **Leo** (July 24–August 23). If you marry when the Sun is in Leo, your marriage will encourage your sense of fun, creative expression, and showmanship—perfect for helping you express your beliefs and vision in an enjoyable and accessible way.

- **Libra** (September 24–October 23). The Libra marriage encourages an exchange of views and respect for other ways of thinking. This is a healthy influence for Sagittarius, who can sometimes have a hard time entertaining other ideas and viewpoints.

- **Sagittarius** (November 23–December 21). Your Sun-in-Sagittarius marriage will fan the flames of your natural exuberance and philosophical nature. This is comfortable for you, but it may not provide sufficient checks and balances to offer different perspectives and viewpoints.

- **Aquarius** (January 21–February 18). The Sun-in-Aquarius marriage is a wonderful match for you, lightening your philosophical side with a certain wackiness and love of freedom. It also tends to pair you with a partner who is your equal in every way, which helps you keep your own importance in perspective.

If You Were Born with the Sun in Capricorn

Born in the quiet of winter, your life's path is an uphill climb toward achievement and respect. To balance your need to accomplish goals, even at the expense of your own comfort, you unconsciously seek partners who provide the nurturing support you need to sustain you in your climb. Capricorn men tend to seek partners who enjoy creating a welcoming nest and tending to human relationships; Capricorn women are attracted to partners who appreciate their worldliness and do not feel threatened by it. Both sexes do best in a marriage that provides an atmosphere that balances outer-world ambition with the comfort and connection of a warm home life.

BEST MARRIAGE SIGNS FOR CAPRICORN

- **Taurus** (April 21–May 21). Marrying while the Sun is in Taurus is marvelous for you, as your marriage tends to encourage you to relax a little and enjoy life's simple pleasures. You may occasionally feel, however, as though the relaxed pace of your marriage removes some of the edge that you need in order to compete in a tough world.

- **Cancer** (June 22–July 23). The Sun-in-Cancer marriage focuses on family building instead of career building. For this reason, it represents a good environment for balancing the extremes of your personality, but may also cause a certain amount of conflict as you struggle to balance your ambitious nature with the demands of a full home life.

- **Virgo** (August 24–September 23). A marriage with the Sun in Virgo emphasizes qualities of practicality and service that are very compatible with your own pragmatism. It is a marriage that will encourage humility and the desire to be useful—very good characteristics for keeping you from indulging Capricorn's authoritarian dark side.

- **Scorpio** (October 24–November 22). A marriage that begins with the Sun in Scorpio awakens passion and deep emotional connection. While this might feel a bit uncomfortable for practical Capricorn, it can bring an extremely exciting, even magical dimension to your life that will be most welcome.

- **Capricorn** (December 22–January 20). A marriage with the Sun in Capricorn encourages you and your partner to pursue your worldly ambitions without impediment and to give back to your community. This is a marriage that will help you succeed beyond your wildest expectations, but it may not provide the emotional balance and passionate connection of a Cancer or Scorpio marriage.

- **Pisces** (February 18–March 20). The Sun-in-Pisces marriage seeks an atmosphere of gentle contemplation, compassion, and spiritual exploration. While this sounds—and is!—quite different from your nature and goals, the Sun-in-Pisces marriage can complement your worldly objectives with a feeling of connection to other people and a sense of spiritual purpose.

If You Were Born with the Sun in Aquarius

Your life's path compels you to **be a revolutionary**, breaking away from old structures and traditions. To prevent you from becoming too isolated from the rest of the human race, you unconsciously seek partners who are outgoing and who thrive on human connections and approval. The Aquarius man seeks a partner who is proud, dignified, and charismatic; the Aquarius woman is fascinated by charming, attractive partners with sex appeal. Both sexes do best in a marriage that combines independence with camaraderie, cool detachment with warmth and magnetism.

BEST MARRIAGE SIGNS FOR AQUARIUS

- **Aries** (March 21–April 20). The Sun-in-Aries marriage is as revolutionary as you are, amplifying your natural urge to blaze new trails and upset the apple cart of traditional thinking. There is little in this marriage to temper your antisocial side, though, so you will need to find other ways to forge warmer connections with your fellow man.

- **Gemini** (May 22–June 21). The marriage that begins with the Sun in Gemini helps bring out your clever, quick-witted side. You can be prone to gloominess, and your Gemini marriage will distract you from your moods with new people, places, and ideas.

- **Leo** (July 24–August 23). A marriage with the Sun in Leo is one of the better choices for you, as it emphasizes the warm, personal connections and sense of fun that you sometimes lack. Your partner may drag you kicking and screaming to social engagements, but like good medicine, it will be just what the doctor ordered.

- **Libra** (September 24–October 23). The Sun-in-Libra marriage encourages the art of tactful give-and-take with others, a skill you often eschew in favor of the "shock and awe" approach to interaction. You are a revolutionary thinker, and your Sun-in-Libra marriage will help you find a wider audience for your ideas by tempering your wild, eccentric side.

- **Sagittarius** (November 23–December 21). Your Sun-in-Sagittarius marriage creates an environment that supports freedom, independence, and abstract thinking. These are traits you already possess in abundance, so this marriage will be comfortable but will not particularly challenge you to develop complementary traits.

- **Aquarius** (January 21–February 18). The Sun-in-Aquarius marriage is a union of strong individuals who pursue their own goals in an atmosphere of mutual support. Your marriage will support both your best traits and your weaknesses, offering little balance for your often reckless tendencies.

If You Were Born with the Sun in Pisces

Born in late winter's thaw, your life's mission is to dissolve boundaries between yourself and other people and immerse yourself in life's mysteries. To balance your sensitivity and vulnerability, you unconsciously seek partners who evaluate others with a more discerning eye. Pisces men and women alike tend to seek partners who are gifted critical thinkers and who have the ability to navigate the practical problems of the real world. Both sexes do best in a marriage that balances compassion and sensitivity with discernment and practicality.

BEST MARRIAGE SIGNS FOR PISCES

- **Taurus** (April 21–May 21). The stable and practical Sun-in-Taurus marriage is one of your best marriage sign choices. You are a sensitive sort who struggles a bit with life's practical realities, and the Taurus marriage will provide a grounding and steady foundation for your otherworldly flights of fancy.

- **Cancer** (June 22–July 23). The Sun-in-Cancer marriage encourages the soulful emotionalism that is second nature to you. The Cancerian focus on the family may occasionally feel limiting to someone like you, whose compassion extends far beyond the bounds of your own household, but it also provides a sense of direction and purpose that Pisces may sometimes lack.

- **Virgo** (August 24–September 23). Virgo is your most complementary marriage sign. You may occasionally feel criticized and critical, and your spiritual side overshadowed by mundane concerns such as paying the power bill; but this marriage encourages your growth by focusing you on the critical judgment and practical life skills that you prefer to leave to others.

- **Scorpio** (October 24–November 22). A marriage that begins with the Sun in Scorpio amplifies your intuitive and sensitive side, but it also demands full-time passion and intimacy with one other person, which may occasionally feel overwhelming for you.

- **Capricorn** (December 22–January 20). The Sun-in-Capricorn marriage provides an atmosphere of ambition, pragmatism, and achievement that can help you transform your compassion and caring into real-world philanthropy and service.

- **Pisces** (February 19–March 20). The Sun-in-Pisces marriage is one that matches your desire for meditation and spiritual outreach. As long as the two of you can encourage each other to attend to real-world concerns as needed, so that the laundry is washed and the bills paid, it can be a haven of peace and enlightenment for you.

Happily Ever After…

A newspaper clipping of a cartoon hangs on my refrigerator door, a gift from a mischievous friend who admires both my cats and my marriage. Two cartoon cats observe a living room full of shredded draperies, carpeting, and furniture. One cat, beaming with obvious pride, tells the other, "It's been a lot of hard work, but the house is finally starting to feel like mine!"

After fourteen years of marriage, I have some idea how that cat feels. Even if you marry precisely the right person, at a moment endorsed by all the heavens, it takes awhile to make a marriage feel "lived in." Even the best houses have quirks, nooks and crannies that we discover over time and learn to treasure, even if they occasionally aggravate us.

The same is true of a marriage. Individually, each of you must scratch out your own territory; as a team, you'll learn to share, to compromise, and to row your boats in the same direction. There are no shortcuts to living happily ever after—it all takes time, love, and patience. But delightful rewards and intriguing mysteries await you on your journey. *Bon voyage!*

LLEWELLYN ORDERING INFORMATION

Order Online:
Visit our website at www.llewellyn.com, select your books, and order them on our secure server.

Order by Phone:
- Call toll-free within the U.S. at 1-877-NEW-WRLD (1-877-639-9753). Call toll-free within Canada at 1-866-NEW-WRLD (1-866-639-9753)
- We accept VISA, MasterCard, and American Express

Order by Mail:
Send the full price of your order (MN residents add 7% sales tax) in U.S. funds, plus postage & handling to:

> **Llewellyn Worldwide**
> **2143 Wooddale Drive, Dept. 978-0-7387-1169-0**
> **Woodbury, MN 55125-2989, U.S.A.**

Postage & Handling:

Standard (U.S., Mexico, & Canada). If your order is:
$24.99 and under, add $3.00
$25.00 and over, FREE STANDARD SHIPPING

AK, HI, PR: $15.00 for one book plus $1.00 for each additional book.

International Orders (airmail only):
$16.00 for one book plus $3.00 for each additional book

Orders are processed within 2 business days.
Please allow for normal shipping time. Postage and handling rates subject to change.

Star Guide to Guys

How to Live Happily With Him . . .
or Without Him

ELIZABETH PERKINS

Elizabeth Perkins dishes the dirt on men in all twelve Sun signs—covering their strengths, challenges, goals, desires, and other personality traits. Women can also depend on this entertaining, easy-to-use guide for insight into their own sign: what they're looking for in a mate, relationship needs, and compatibility with each sign. There's also astrological advice for living a fabulous single life.

978-0-7387-0954-3
6 x 9, 240 pp. $12.95

Spanish edition:
Cómo vivir con él ... o sin él
978-0-7387-1069-3 $13.95

To order, call 1-877-NEW-WRLD
Prices subject to change without notice

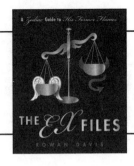

The Ex Files

A Zodiac Guide to His Former Flames

ROWAN DAVIS

If your guy's ex is driving you crazy, check out this fun astrological guide to figuring her out. From vain Leos to secretive Scorpios, *The Ex Files* dishes the dirt on all twelve Sun signs and gives insight into what you can expect from each. There's also advice—based on your own Sun sign—for coping with a variety of exes.

978-0-7387-1044-0

5 x 6, 216 pp. $12.95

The Ex-Boyfriend Book

A Zodiac Guide to Your Former Flames

ROWAN DAVIS

Astrologically sound, yet irresistibly cheeky, *The Ex-Boyfriend Book* helps ladies answer the complicated questions that follow a breakup: What went wrong? Can we stay friends? Why was I ever attracted to that freak? Revealing cosmic insights into your ex's personality, this laugh-out-loud book will help you make sense of your romantic past.

978-0-7387-1143-0
5 x 6, 216 pp. $12.95

Cosmic Trends

Astrology Connects the Dots

PHILIP BROWN

According to Philip Brown, trends in technology, film, books, TV, music, and fashion are all influenced by planetary movement. *Cosmic Trends* discusses the startling impact Pluto, Neptune, and Uranus have had—and continue to have—on our evolving culture. Fascinating forecasts and a glimpse of what to expect in 2020 are also included.

978-0-7387-0992-5
6 x 9, 264 pp. $14.95

To order, call 1-877-NEW-WRLD
Prices subject to change without notice

Feng Shui in 5 Minutes

SELENA SUMMERS

Written in a conversational question-and-answer format, this insightful guide provides intriguing no-cost methods to improve your luck, a mystic way to hurry house sales, ancient techniques to win more dates, the Nine Celestial Cures, common feng shui faults, and much more. It's the only feng shui book to reveal Yin moonlight and Yang daylight lucky charms for all birth years.

978-0-7387-0291-9
5 ³⁄₁₆ x 8, 240 pp. $12.95

Spanish edition:
Feng Shui práctico y al instante
978-0-7387-0292-6 $12.95

To order, call 1-877-NEW-WRLD
Prices subject to change without notice

The Power of Time

*Understanding the Cycles of
Your Life's Path*

PAULINE EDWARD

Develop a successful life plan and take advantage of the natural cycles influencing your life. Simple calculations based on numerology (derived from a birth date) will reveal where you are in each nine-year cycle and what to expect from each year, month, and day. Discover the best times to start a new job, focus on family, launch a business, and more.

978-0-7387-1149-2
7 ½ x 9 ⅛, 240 pp. $15.95

Abundance for Beginners

Simple Strategies for Successful Living

ELLEN PETERSON

Whatever success means to you—the perfect job, a loving spouse, financial security—it's all possible. This book teaches you how to trust in the Universe and find the path to self-fulfillment. Ellen Peterson explores the power of spirituality, positive thoughts, generosity, and integrity. You'll also learn to use visualization, spoken words, and positive intention to achieve your heart's desires.

978-0-7387-0770-9
5 ³/₁₆ x 8, 240 pp. $12.95

Spanish edition:
Abriendo Camino a la Abundancia
978-0-7387-1076-1 $13.95

To order, call 1-877-NEW-WRLD
Prices subject to change without notice

Friends and Lovers Astrology Relationship Reading:
Personal Astrology Report $20

Every relationship contains points of similarity and harmony as well as points of conflict and discord. Because each of us has a unique astrological chart based on position of the planets and houses at the moment of our births, an astrologer can reveal the many different ways that two people relate with each other by comparing and contrasting the interrelationships of two separate charts. Practiced for several thousand years, this is the art of *synastry*.

Our thorough and professional report analyzes each of the two selected charts and interprets the astrological connections between them, with four possible sections, two for each of the charts. For each individual the two possible sections are: (1) How this person approaches relationships. (2) How this person relates specifically with the second person.

Using in-depth astrological reports you can learn how to cultivate and encourage the positive and harmonious within your relationships, and keep them growing and fruitful through the highs and lows of the passing years.

To order or for more information please contact us at 1-877-NEW-WRLD. *Please allow 2-4 weeks for your chart to be processed.*

To Write to the Author

If you wish to contact the author or would like more information about this book, please write to the author in care of Llewellyn Worldwide and we will forward your request. Both the author and publisher appreciate hearing from you and learning of your enjoyment of this book and how it has helped you. Llewellyn Worldwide cannot guarantee that every letter written to the author can be answered, but all will be forwarded. Please write to:

April Elliott Kent
℅ Llewellyn Worldwide
2143 Wooddale Drive, Dept. 978-0-7387-1169-0
Woodbury, MN 55125-2989, U.S.A.
Please enclose a self-addressed stamped envelope for reply,
or $1.00 to cover costs. If outside U.S.A., enclose
international postal reply coupon.

Many of Llewellyn's authors have websites with additional information and resources. For more information, please visit our website at:
www.llewellyn.com